The Book of
Great
One-
liners

Jenny Hunter

NEW
HOLLAND

First published in Australia in 2006 by
New Holland Publishers (Australia) Pty Ltd
Sydney • Auckland • London • Cape Town

14 Aquatic Drive Frenchs Forest NSW 2086 Australia
218 Lake Road Northcote Auckland New Zealand
86 Edgware Road London W2 2EA United Kingdom
80 McKenzie Street Cape Town 8001 South Africa

National Library of Australia Cataloguing-in-Publication Data:
Hunter, Jenny, 1955- .

The book of great one-liners.

ISBN(13) 978-1-74110-420-2

1. Epigrams - Humour. 2. Aphorisms and apothegms - Humour.
3. Quotations - Humour. 4. Wit and humour. I. Title.

808.882

Publisher: Fiona Schultz
Managing Editor: Martin Ford
Designer: Tania Gomes
Project Editor: Lliane Clarke
Production: Grace Gutwein
Printer: Griffin Press, Adelaide

10 9 8 7 6 5 4 3

Acknowledgements

Thanks to my friends and relatives for their suggestions, ideas and encouragement during my research. I hope you recognise your suggestions. Particular thanks to the McTaggarts (for summer hospitality and fresh perspectives), Simon (for loads of ideas and the intro), and Fergie (for being Fergie and, mostly, staying out of my hair).

For Andrew Francis McTaggart, 1982-2005

Life changes fast.
Life changes in an instant.
You sit down to dinner and life as you know it ends.
Joan Didion

Contents

Introduction

Which one-liners should you choose to be in a book like this? Certainly, one-liners should be clever. They should be witty, probably showing quick wit. They should be brief (but not necessarily literally one line). They should be effective (now we start to get into a grey area); funny (more grey); original (very grey).

'Effective' is often in the eye of the beholder, or beholden. And there are many categories of effective: effective at cutting someone down; effective in offering a point of view; effective in ending a joke, scene or conversation.

'Funny' is even more subjective. Because many people only have knowledge in some subjects, or have had serious humour-bypass operations, or are just slow—what is side-splitting for some may well be missed by some or, worse, unfunny and offensive for others. Billy Connolly, for example, uses four-letter words frequently and, for some people, this interferes with their ability to appreciate his material.

'Original' is even harder. Who's to say who said it first, and in what exact form? A comedian or debater may well create a line and be the first to use it, but very often may have been given it; or may have 'borrowed' it and is merely the first to state it in a memorable context, and have it recorded for the first time.

Sometimes a one-liner's success is in the delivery and sense of timing of the person saying the lines. Bob Hope was famous for his sense of timing when delivering a comedy routine. He breaks the 'original' rule which he acknowledges with a one-liner, 'You wouldn't get away with that if my scriptwriter was here'.

Actors, comedians and speech-makers very often work from a script, so the words are not 'theirs'. But someone—the scriptwriter, the speechwriter, a friend—thought of them. And while it is not always 'spontaneous' in the context of the delivery, or an 'original' line of the deliverer, the one-liner is witty and clever and brief and deserves being acknowledged.

A one-liner can be a quip, rejoinder, interjection, serious observation, or thought. It can be a part of a script, stand-up routine, interview, conversation, speech, or writing. Often, it is in glorious isolation.

So the 'rules' are subjective and problematic, and often broken, especially in the case of bloopers, and vividly ignorant comments—they are not intentionally clever, just brief and funny.

I hope you enjoy this selection, and that some of the one-liners leave you with the thought, 'I wish I'd said that'.

Simon Balderstone

Ability, Ambition and Aspiration

If life were fair, Dan Quayle would be making a living asking 'Do you want fries with that?'
John Cleese, English comedian, actor and writer

I'm not offended by all the dumb-blonde jokes because I know that I'm not dumb. I also know I'm not blonde.
Dolly Parton, American singer and actor

She couldn't edit a bus ticket.
Kelvin Mackenzie, English tabloid newspaper editor, about Janet Street-Porter's appointment as a BBC editor

I didn't go into the water, I just walked across it.
Gough Whitlam, Australian prime minister, when asked what the water was like following a swim

My mother, Margaret, was a Commonwealth Games swimmer and my father, Gough, could walk on water.
Nick Whitlam, Gough and Margaret Whitlam's son, about his swimming ability

A lot of fellows nowadays have a BA, MD, or PhD. Unfortunately, they don't have a J-O-B.
Fats Domino, American singer

Eddy: In Zen terms we are all just molecules. There's no difference between me and the table, me and a tree, me and Madonna.
Saffy: Except you have a fatter bottom.
Absolutely Fabulous

There are three kinds of people: those who count and those who don't.

In America, anyone can become president. That's the problem.
George Carlin, American actor and comedian

Democracy means that anyone can grow up to be president, and anyone who doesn't grow up can be vice president.

I've seen him entertain fifty times and I've always enjoyed his joke.
Johnny Carson (1925-2005), American chat-show host

Harry Truman proves that old adage that any man can become president of the United States.
Norman Thomas (1884-1968), American politician

I have nothing to declare except my genius.
Oscar Wilde (1854-1900), Irish-born writer, to US customs

My information was that he had a plastic hose, a canary and a geranium and they made him Minister for Primary Industries.
Fred Daly (1913-95), Labor Party politician, about Billy McMahon who was (briefly) Australian prime minister

Never try to keep up with the Joneses...drag them down to your level. It's cheaper.
Quentin Crisp (1908-99), English-born writer and gay icon

Whatever women do, they must do twice as well as men to be thought half as good. Luckily, this is not difficult.
Charlotte Whitton (1896-1975), Canadian feminist and politician

Be like a postage stamp. Stick to one thing until you get there.
Josh Billings (1815-85), American humorist

A self-made man? Yes, and one who worships his creator.
William Cowper (1731-1800), English poet (Used by others including John Bright about Benjamin Disraeli)

Ability, Ambition and Aspiration

Ageing

If you must lie about your age, do it in the other direction: tell people you're 97 and they'll think you look fucking great.

In a certain light, my willie looks like Stewart Granger.
Billy Connolly, Scottish comedian and actor, about his greying pubic hair (Granger was a swashbuckling, romantic, leading man from the 40's and 50's who had a healthy head of greying hair.)

Over at News Limited, this must be sending Rupert Murdoch white with worry. Except that as we saw from the pictures at his annual general meeting, his hair seems to have turned prematurely chestnut.
Mike Carlton, Australian journalist and radio broadcaster

At my age I do what Mark Twain did. I get my daily paper, look at the obituaries page and if I'm not there I carry on as usual.
Patrick Moore, English astronomer

Mother: What is my email address?
Eddy: oldwoman@risk-of-being-strangled-by-own-daughter.com, I should imagine.
Absolutely Fabulous

A lot of people don't think I know the meaning of the word 'hip'. I do, and hope to have it replaced very soon.
Terry Wogan, British chat-show host

Remember that as a teenager you are at the last stage in your life when you will be happy to hear that the phone is for you.
Fran Lebowitz, American author

You can live to be a hundred if you give up all the things that make you want to live to be a hundred.
Woody Allen, American comedian, actor and film director

When you get to my age, life seems little more than one long march to and from the lavatory.
John Mortimer, British barrister and writer, from his novel *Summer's Lease*

I remember one of my staff asking me when I was going to retire. I said when I could no longer hear the sound of laughter. He said, 'That never stopped you before'.

She said she was approaching 40 and I couldn't help wondering from what direction.

Middle age is when your age starts to show around the middle.
Bob Hope (1903-2003), American comedian and actor

All that I know I learned after I was thirty.
Georges Clemenceau (1841-1929), French prime minister

I am not young enough to know everything.
J M Barrie (1860-1937), Scottish writer and author of *Peter Pan*

The old believe everything; the middle-aged suspect everything; the young know everything.
Oscar Wilde (1854-1900), Irish-born writer

Middle age: When you're sitting at home on Saturday night and the telephone rings and you hope it isn't for you.
Ogden Nash (1902-71), American poet and humorist

Youth is a wonderful thing. What a crime to waste it on children.
George Bernard Shaw (1856-1960), Irish playwright and Nobel Prize winner

To me old age is always fifteen years older than I am.
Bernard Baruch (1870-1965), American financier and political adviser

I never think of the future. It comes soon enough.
Albert Einstein (1879-1955), German-born physicist and Nobel Prize winner

I try to wear my scarf so tightly fixed under my chin that it holds in place the loose flesh there, and conceals my crumbling facade.

Quentin Crisp (1908-99), English-born writer and gay icon

First you forget names, then you forget faces. Next you forget to pull your zipper up and, finally, you forget to pull it down.

George Burns (1896-1996), American comedian

A dead bird does not leave its nest.

Winston Churchill (1874-1965), British prime minister, when told in his later years that his fly was undone

---

Robbins: I've just written my 87th book.
Cartland: I've written 145.
Robbins: Oh, I see, one a year.

Denise Robbins and Barbara Cartland are authors of romance fiction

Awards, Honours and Royalty

Please don't recount this vote.
Al Gore, US vice president and 2000 presidential candidate, in an acceptance speech which had a limit of five words. The 2000 presidential election was delayed by the recounting of votes from Florida and the Supreme Court decided to stop the recount at a point when George W Bush was ahead

They look far too *outré* anywhere else. They're great big, gold, shiny things. They're up there tarnishing quietly along with everything else I own, including my body.
Emma Thompson, English actor, about why she keeps her Oscars in her bedroom

Awards are like piles. Sooner or later, every bum gets one.
Maureen Lipman, English actor

She's head of a dysfunctional family—if she lived on a council estate in Sheffield, she'd probably be in council care.
Michael Parkinson, English chat-show host, about Queen Elizabeth II

The *eminence cerise*, the bolster behind the throne.
Will Self, English writer, about Elizabeth the Queen Mother

To be Prince of Wales is not a position. It is a predicament.
Alan Bennett, English playwright, from the film, *The Madness of King George*

I'm prepared to take advice on leisure from Prince Philip. He's a world expert on leisure. He's been practising for most of his adult life.
Neil Kinnock, British Labour politician

I think everyone really will concede that on this, of all days, I should begin my speech with the words 'My husband and I'.
Queen Elizabeth II, about her 25th wedding anniversary

When I appear in public people expect me to neigh, grind my teeth, paw the ground and swish my tail.
Princess Anne, ninth in line to the British throne

Prince Charles is planning to record his own version of Frank Sinatra's hit, 'My Way'. He's going to call it 'One Did It One's Way'.
Neil Shand, English comedian

Upper crust—a lot of crumbs held together with dough.
Graffiti from University of Newcastle (UK)

One day there will only be five kings left: hearts, spades, diamonds, clubs and England.
King Farouk of Egypt (1920-65)

I'm proud to have joined the ranks of Australian Legends ... including Don Bradman. I'm told he was very good but I don't know a lot about football.
Dame Edna Everage, Australian housewife superstar, who was named a 2006 Australian Legend and had a set of postage stamps printed in her honour

They're going to be lickable and self-adhesive…every man's dream.
Barry Humphries, Dame Edna's creator, about the quality of his Australian Legend postage stamp

Ernie: My name is colonel Napoleon Davenport, DSO, MC, OBE.
Eric: That's a funny way to spell Davenport.
Morecambe and Wise

He had hidden shallows.
Clive James, Australian-born writer, about King Edward VIII

After a very long year, we've got a very short knight.
David Lange (1942-2005), New Zealand prime minister, about Robert Muldoon's knighthood

It's not a high-class escort agency.
David Lange, about being made a Companion of Honour

The Oscars are two hours of sparkling entertainment packed into a four-hour show.
Johnny Carson (1925-2005), American chat-show host

I'm glad to see that the royalty here tonight is not only confined to the Royal Box.
Dusty Springfield (1939-99), English singer, at a concert at London's Albert Hall. Princess Margaret was in the Royal Box and the audience was packed with gay people. When her escorts explained the joke, Princess Margaret walked out

> ***Ernie:*** Are you of royal stock?
> ***Eric:*** No, my father was a grocer. I'm of vegetable stock.
> *Morecambe and Wise*

Beauty, Style and Fashion

If I had been around when Rubens was painting, I would have been revered as a fabulous model. Kate Moss? Well, she would have been the paintbrush.

Dawn French, English comedian and actor

You'll be silicone from tits to toenails.

I've got enough crows' feet to start a bird sanctuary.

Kathy Lette, Australian-born writer, *Nip 'n' Tuck*

Darling, if that woman has one more face lift she'll have a beard.

If models get any younger, they'll be throwing foetuses down the catwalk.

Patsy Stone, ageing model from *Absolutely Fabulous*

I'm not like you, Saff. I can't go around smelling like an old bowl of porridge, can I sweetie?

Everything you wear looks like it's bearing a grudge.

I can't give away my old clothes to the poor. They have enough to put up with without the added humiliation of wearing last season.

Edina Monsoon, to her daughter Saffy, from *Absolutely Fabulous*

A narcissist is someone better looking than you are.

Gore Vidal, American writer and satirist

Your right to wear a mint-green polyester leisure suit ends where it meets my eye.

If you are a dog and your owner suggests that you wear a sweater...suggest that he wear a tail.
Fran Lebowitz, American author

Do you know how many polyesters died to make that shirt?
Steve Martin, American comedian and actor

It takes up to 40 dumb animals to make a fur coat but only one to wear it.
1980s anti-fur slogan

There we were in the middle of a sexual revolution wearing clothes that guaranteed we wouldn't get laid.
Denis Leary, American comedian and actor

Beggar: Ma'am, I haven't eaten in three days.
Woman: Gee, I sure wish I had your willpower.
From a Bob Hope routine

...it is possible, even today, for a man to climb a long way in Australian society while being no better groomed than the Man from Snowy River's horse...
Clive James, Australian-born writer

The leading cause of death among fashion models is falling through street grates.
Dave Barry, *Miami Herald* columnist

Beauty is only a light switch away.
Austin Powers, character from the movie *Austin Powers*

I joined a health club last year and spent about £400, but I didn't lose a pound. Apparently you have to turn up.
Jo Brand, English comedian

I'm on so many pills I'll need a childproof lid on my coffin.
Paul O'Grady, English comedian

In Hollywood, people are going for plastic surgery at 23. I'm going to wait until there is enough spare skin to make a handbag and matching gloves.
Pam Ferris, British actress

A lot of people are into body piercing. They end up looking like they've been mugged by a staple gun.
Robin Williams, American comedian and actor

Men who have a pierced ear are better prepared for marriage. They've experienced pain and bought jewellery.
Rita Rudner, American comedian

Oh my goodness, she has a chandelier in her navel.
June Dally-Watkins, Australian businesswoman and former Australian model of the year, about pierced navels

It has been said that a pretty face is a passport. But it's not, it's a visa, and it runs out fast.
Julie Burchill, British writer

The problem with beauty is that it's like being born rich and getting progressively poorer.
Joan Collins, English-born actor

A woman went to a plastic surgeon and asked him to make her like Bo Derek. He gave her a lobotomy.
Joan Rivers, American comedian

I comfort myself by pretending the number on my bathroom scales is my IQ.
Linda Iverson

Beauty comes in all sizes, not just size five.
Roseanne Barr, American comedian

There's so much plastic in this culture that vinyl leopard skin is becoming an endangered synthetic.
Lily Tomlin, American actress and comedian

Nudity is a deep worry if you have a body like a bin bag full of yoghurt.
Stephen Fry, English actor and writer

Haute couture should be fun, foolish and almost unwearable.
Christian Lacroix, French couturier

An optimist is a girl who mistakes a bulge for a curve.
Ring Lardner (1885-1933), American sportswriter

It's not true that I had nothing on. I had the radio on.
Marilyn Monroe (1926-62), American actor, sex symbol and pop icon

Fashion may be stylish, but it is not style. Fashion is instead of style.
Quentin Crisp (1908-99), English-born writer and gay icon

She got her looks from her father. He's a plastic surgeon.
Groucho Marx (1890-1977), American comedian and actor

My wife had plastic surgery. I cut up all her credit cards.
Henny Youngman (1906-98), American comedian, given the title 'King of the One-Liners' by Walter Winchell

The Right Hon was a tubby little chap who looked as if he had been poured into his clothes and had forgotten to say 'When!'
P G Wodehouse (1881-1975), English-born writer

Eddy: Inside of me, sweetie, inside of me, there is a thin person just screaming to get out.
Mother: Just the one, dear?
Absolutely Fabulous

The last time I saw anything like that on a top lip, the whole herd had to be destroyed.
Eric Morecambe (1926-84), English comedian, and part of the double act, Morecambe and Wise

If you want to see the girl next door, go next door.
Joan Crawford (1905-77), American actress

Sometimes I can't figure designers out. It's as if they flunked human anatomy.

In two decades I've lost a total of 789 pounds. I should be hanging from a charm bracelet.

The only reason I would take up jogging is so that I could hear heavy breathing again.
Erma Bombeck (1927-96), American writer

The trick of wearing mink is to look as though you were wearing a cloth coat. The trick of wearing a cloth coat is to look as though you are wearing mink.
Pierre Balmain (1914-82), French couturier

Fashion changes, style remains.
Coco Chanel (1883-1971), French couturier

You know you're ugly when you go to the proctologist and he sticks his finger in your mouth.
Rodney Dangerfield (1921-2004), American comedian and actor

Your best side? My dear, you're sitting on it.
Alfred Hitchcock (1899-1980), British-born film director

Being Human

But enough about me. Let's talk about you. What do you think of me?
Bette Midler, American singer, actor and comedian

I rationalise shop. I think a lot of women do that. Like, I buy a dress because I need change for gum.
Rita Rudner, American comedian

Sure thing, man. I used to be a laboratory myself once.
Keith Richards, Rolling Stones, when asked to autograph a school chemistry book

I'm really running out of excuses with this guy. I need some kind of excuse Rolodex.
Jerry Seinfeld, American comedian

Life is like a sewer. What you get out of it depends on what you put into it.
Tom Lehrer, American singer and satirist

Computers don't poop, fart, fuck or laugh and cannot detect irony. These, then, are the distinguishing characteristics of humanity.
Eric Idle, English comedian

Most people have a lifeline on the palm of their hand. My wife has a clothes line.
Michael Visontay, Australian journalist, about his wife's shopping

George: People think I'm smart, but I'm not smart.
Jerry: Who thinks you're smart?
Seinfeld

There are no exceptions to the rule that everybody likes to be an exception to the rule.
William F Buckley Jnr, American conservative commentator

He's not unlike Hitler, but without the charm.
Gore Vidal, American writer, about William F Buckley Jnr

A clear conscience is usually the sign of a bad memory.
Steven Wright, American actor, writer and comedian

For sale: Complete set of Encyclopaedia Britannica. No longer required as wife knows everything.
Graffiti seen by Billy Connolly during his *World Tour of New Zealand*

Racism isn't born, folks, it's taught. I have a two-year-old son. You know what he hates? Naps! End of list.
Denis Leary, American comedian and actor

I plan to have character one day. Great character. But if you want to be rich, you better get the money before the scruples set in.
Richard Fish, character from television program, *Ally McBeal*

The good thing about procrastination is that you always have something planned for tomorrow.
Anon

I was thinking of setting up a procrastinator's club but only got as far as the motto: 'Don't just do something, stand there'.
Peter Rosier, *Sydney Morning Herald* letter writer, 18 Jan 2006

An apathy club sounded fun, but I couldn't be bothered.
Warwick Orme, *Sydney Morning Herald* letter writer, 18 Jan 2006

If it weren't for the last minute, nothing would get done.
Anon

Never go to bed mad. Stay up and fight.
Phyllis Diller, American comedian

Too bad all the people who know how to run the country are busy driving cabs and cutting hair.
George Burns (1896-1996), American comedian

Every time I look at you I get a fierce desire to be lonesome.
Oscar Levant (1906-72), American musician, comedian and writer

Always back the horse called self-interest, son. It'll be the only one trying.
Jack Lang (1876-1975), NSW premier

Those are my principles. If you don't like them I have others.
Groucho Marx (1890-1977), American comedian and actor

Flattery is like cologne water; to be smelt of, not swallowed.
Josh Billings (1815-85), American humorist

There are three roads to ruin; women, gambling and technicians. The most pleasant is with women, the quickest is with gambling but the surest is with technicians.
Georges Pompidou (1911-74), French president

I spent a lot of my money on booze, birds and fast cars—the rest I just squandered.
George Best (1946-2005), Northern Irish-born footballer, who died of liver failure at age 59

Sir Humphrey: There is no reason to change a system which has worked so well in the past.
Hacker: But it hasn't.
Sir Humphrey: But we've got to give the present system a fair trial.
Hacker: Ah yes, I thought you might say that. It may interest you to know, Humphrey, that the Most Noble Order of the Garter was founded in 1348 by King Edward III. I think perhaps it may be coming towards the end of its trial period now, don't you?
Yes Minister

In 1969 I gave up women and alcohol—it was the worst 20 minutes of my life.
George Best

Hacker: Humphrey, do you see it as part of your job to help ministers make fools of themselves?
Sir Humphrey: Well, I never met one that needed any help.
Yes Minister

A neurosis is a secret that you don't know you are keeping.
Kenneth Tynan (1927-80), English theatre critic

Forgive your enemies, but never forget their names.
John F Kennedy (1917-63), US president

People who fly into a rage always make a bad landing.
Will Rogers (1879-1935), American entertainer

The graveyards are full of indispensable men.
Charles de Gaulle (1890-1970), French military leader and president (also attributed to Georges Clemenceau)

Rookwood Cemetery is full of indispensable men.
Joseph Chifley (1885-1951), Australian prime minister (an Australian variation of de Gaulle's)

Never explain—your friends do not need it and your enemies will not believe you anyhow.
Elbert Hubbard (1856-1915), American writer

I've been on a calendar, but I've never been on time.
Marilyn Monroe (1926-62), American actor, sex symbol and pop icon

If A is a success in life, then A equals x plus y plus z. Work is x; y is play; and z is keeping your mouth shut.
Albert Einstein (1879-1955), German-born physicist and Nobel Prize winner

An optimist sees an opportunity in every calamity; a pessimist sees a calamity in every opportunity.

Winston Churchill (1874-1965), English prime minister

Nine-tenths of the people were created so you would want to be with the other tenth.

Horace Walpole (1717-97), English writer and politician

Shaw: Reserving two tickets for you for my premiere. Come and and bring a friend—if you have one.
Churchill: Impossible to be present for first performance. Will attend the second—if there is one.

A written exchange between George Bernard Shaw and Winston Churchill

The better I get to know men, the more I find myself loving dogs.

Charles de Gaulle (1890-1970), French military leader and president

Why do boys play with balls? Probably it's the first thing they've got hold of when they wake up.

Ted Whitten (1933-95), Australian football legend

Show me a man who is a good loser and I'll show you a man who's playing golf with his boss.

Jim Murray (1919-98), American sports journalist and Pulitzer Prize winner

People who begin sentences with 'I may be old-fashioned but ...' are usually not only old-fashioned but wrong.

Robert Benchley (1889-1945), American writer, actor and member of the Round Table

Heckler: Death to the idiots!
de Gaulle: That's a tall order, indeed.

Charles de Gaulle

Business, Leadership and Power

Rupert's idea of a better world is a world that's better for Rupert.
Ted Turner, founder of CNN, about Rupert Murdoch.

I find it rather easy to portray a businessman. Being bland, rather cruel, and incompetent comes naturally to me.
John Cleese, English comedian and actor

Trickle-down theory—the less than elegant metaphor that if one feeds the horse enough oats, some will pass through to the road for the sparrows.
J K Galbraith, Canadian-born American economist

Meetings are an addictive, highly self-indulgent activity that corporations and other large organisations habitually engage in only because they cannot actually masturbate.
Dave Barry, *Miami Herald* columnist

At a Las Vegas casino, Packer queried why someone was getting a lot of attention from staff and was told he was an oilman worth $100 million.
Packer (feigning an impressed tone): Really? $100 million?
Oilman: Yes, I am, sir.
Packer: I'll toss you for it.

Fred got the goldmine, we got the shaft.
A placard at a 2005 journalists' protest outside the annual general meeting of their employer, Fairfax Ltd, about the generous golden handshake of the outgoing chairman

Why have a dog and bark yourself?
Robert T Balderstone, Victorian farmer, about a boss's inability to delegate

You only get one Alan Bond in your lifetime. And I've had mine.
Kerry Packer (1937-2005), Australian businessman. Packer sold the Nine television network to Alan Bond in 1987 for $1 billion and bought it back three years later for $250 million

No self-respecting fish would be wrapped in a Murdoch newspaper.
Mike Royko (1932-97) American journalist, following his resignation from the *Chicago Sun-Times* after it was bought by Rupert Murdoch

There are two things I should tell you about me, son—one, I'm bloody hard to kill and, two, I'm a gambler and I usually win.
Kerry Packer (1937-2005), Australian businessman

A self-made man is one who believes in luck and sends his son to Oxford.
Christina Stead (1902-83), Australian writer

The proofreader of the Revolution is Robespierre. He checked everything, he corrected everything.
Victor Hugo (1802-85), French writer, about the dominant role of Maximilien Robespierre in the French Revolution

Libby was indicted on two counts of perjury and one count of not being as smart as Karl Rove.
Jon Stewart, American comedian, following grand jury indictment of political adviser Lewis Libby in October 2005

Voter: I wouldn't vote for you if you were the Archangel Gabriel.
Menzies: If I were the Archangel Gabriel, you would not be in my constituency.
Robert Menzies, Australian prime minister

Power? It's like a Dead Sea fruit. When you achieve it, there is nothing there.

Harold Macmillan (1894-1986), British prime minister

When they told me that by the year 2100 women would rule the world, my reply was, 'Still?'

Winston Churchill (1874-1965), British prime minister

The board of directors should be made up of three men—two dead and the other dying.

I am drinking from a cup today. I would like a mug but they are all in the board room.

Tommy Docherty, British football coach

Celebrity, Fame and Gossip

All my life, I always wanted to be somebody. Now I see that I should have been more specific.
Lily Tomlin, American actor and comedian

Celebrity is as addictive and destructive as any drink and I am a recovering celebrity.
Barry Manilow, American singer

When someone follows you all the way to the shop and watches you buy toilet roll, you know your life has changed.
Jennifer Aniston, American actor

For years I could walk the streets unrecognised except by people who thought I was Dustin Hoffman.
Al Pacino, American actor

Reporter: What do you think China should do about Tibet?
Pitt: Who cares what I think China should do? I'm a fucking actor. I'm a grown man who puts on make-up.
Brad Pitt starred in the movie *Seven Years in Tibet*

It's really difficult to get out of gossip columns once you've got in.
Mick Jagger, Rolling Stones lead singer

A celebrity is any well-known TV or movie star who looks like he spends more than two hours working on his hair.
Steve Martin, American comedian and actor

Mary-Kate and Ashley Olsen—they are just like panda bears. Everyone's watching them, waiting to see if they'll survive.
Claire Danes, American actor

Elizabeth Taylor has more chins than the Chinese telephone directory.
Joan Rivers, American comedian

You know Elizabeth Taylor? I heard she is the new ride at Disneyworld.
Patsy Stone, ageing model from *Absolutely Fabulous*

With his womanly voice, stark white skin and Medusa hair, his gash of red lipstick, heavy eyeliner, almost non-existent nose and lopsided face, Jackson was making this appearance in order to scotch all rumours that he is not quite normal.
Craig Brown, *Sunday Times* journalist, about Michael Jackson

Nothing travels faster than the speed of light with the possible exception of bad news.
Douglas Adams (1952-2001), British writer

Gossip is the art of saying nothing in a way that leaves practically nothing unsaid.
Walter Winchell (1897-1972), American journalist who invented the gossip column

History is merely gossip.
Oscar Wilde (1854-1900), Irish-born writer

History: gossip well told.
Elbert Hubbard (1856-1915), American writer

Rivers: Come on, Joan, tell us which husband was the best lover.
Collins: Yours.
Joan Rivers and Joan Collins

Don't confuse fame with success. Madonna is one; Helen Keller is the other.
Erma Bombeck (1927-96), American writer

Champagne

Some of our research went straight to our heads.
Don and Petie Kladstrup, American authors of the book, *Champagne*

Fix me a drink…champagne…anything that will blur reality.
Patsy Stone, ageing model from *Absolutely Fabulous*

Come quickly, I'm drinking stars!
Dom Pérignon (1635-1715), Benedictine monk credited with the invention of champagne, said to fellow monks

I drink champagne when I'm happy and when I am sad. Sometimes I drink it when I'm alone. In company I consider it compulsory. I sip a little if I'm hungry. Otherwise, I don't touch it—unless I'm thirsty.
Lily Bollinger (d 1977), French head of Bollinger

Only the unimaginative can fail to find a reason for drinking champagne.
Oscar Wilde (1854-1900), Irish-born writer

Great love affairs start with champagne and end with tisane.
Honoré de Balzac (1798-1850), French author

In victory you deserve it, in defeat you need it.
Napoleon Bonaparte (1769-1821), French military leader and emperor, who collected Moet champagne on the way to his military campaigns (also attributed to Winston Churchill)

> **Braddock:** Winston, you're drunk.
> **Churchill:** Bessie, you're ugly. But tomorrow I shall be sober.
> An exchange between Bessie Braddock and Winston Churchill

Champagne is the wine of civilisation and the oil of government.
Charles Maurice de Talleyrand-Périgord (1754-1883), French diplomat

Champagne offers a minimum of alcohol and a maximum of companionship.
David Niven (1910-83), British actor

Three be the things I shall never attain: envy, content, and sufficient champagne.
Dorothy Parker (1893-1967), American writer and member of the Round Table

Too much of anything is bad, but too much champagne is just right.
Mark Twain (1835-1910), American writer

Your Majesty, I am extremely sorry. My patriotism stops short at my stomach.
Otto von Bismarck (1815-98), Prussian prime minister, to Kaiser Wilhelm about his preference for French rather than German champagne

Meeting Franklin Roosevelt was like opening your first bottle of champagne; knowing him was like drinking it.

The world's most drinkable address.
Churchill, about Odette Pol Roger's home in Paris (Churchill was famous for his love of champagne and has a Pol Roger vintage named after him)

Remember, gentlemen, it's not just France we're fighting for, it's champagne.
Winston Churchill (1874-1965), British prime minister, rallying his troops during World War I

Q: What do you wear in bed?
Marilyn Monroe: Chanel No 5.

Cheating and Lying

I was thrown out of college for cheating on the metaphysics exam; I looked into the soul of the boy sitting next to me.
Woody Allen, American comedian

I always wanted to be the last guy on earth, just to see if all those women were lying to me.
Ronnie Shakes, American comedian

I'm sure he'll find someone else to be unfaithful to soon.
Jerry Hall, American-born model, about ex-partner Mick Jagger

It's like I tell my wife, 'Marge, it takes two to lie: one to lie and one to listen.'
Homer Simpson, from *The Simpsons*

Marge, don't discourage the boy. Weaselling out of things is important to learn. It's what separates us from the animals … except the weasel.
Homer Simpson

Truman Capote has made lying an art—a minor art.
Gore Vidal, American writer

A broad definition of crime in England is that it is any lower-class activity that is displeasing to the upper class.
David Frost, British television comedian and host

Before you judge a man, walk a mile in his shoes. After that, who cares? He's a mile away and you've got his shoes.
Billy Connolly, Scottish comedian and actor

A boy can learn a lot from a dog—obedience, loyalty and the importance of turning around three times before lying down.
Robert Benchley (1889-1945), American writer and member of the Round Table

Legend: a lie that has attained the dignity of age.
H L Mencken (1880-1956), American journalist and satirist, known as the 'Sage of Baltimore'

Euphemisms are unpleasant truths wearing diplomatic cologne.
Quentin Crisp (1908-99), English-born writer and gay icon

A lie can travel halfway around the world while the truth is putting on its shoes.
Mark Twain (1835-1910), American writer (attributed also to Winston Churchill and used by James Callaghan)

Goldwynisms:
A verbal contract isn't worth the paper it's written on.

Anybody who goes to a psychiatrist ought to have his head examined.
Hollywood film producer Sam Goldwyn who became famous for his confused use of English and created his own class of one-liners.

Communication and Language

Man invented language to satisfy his deep need to complain.
Lily Tomlin, American actor and comedian

First law on holes—when you're in one, stop digging.
Denis Healey, British chancellor of the exchequer

The opposite of talking isn't listening. The opposite of talking is waiting.
Fran Lebowitz, American author

> **Blackadder:** Baldrick, have you no idea what irony is?
> **Baldrick:** Yes, it's like goldy and bronzy only it's made out of iron.
> *Blackadder*

Et cetera—the expression that makes people think you know more than you do.
Herbert Prochnow, American banker, writer and toastmaster

First time I read the dictionary, I thought it was a poem about everything.

I've been reading the dictionary. Turns out the zebra did it.

I just got out of hospital. I was in a speed-reading accident. I hit a bookmark.
Steven Wright, American actor, writer and comedian

My wife is teaching me Cuban. It's like Spanish but with fewer words for luxury goods.
Emo Philips, American actor and comedian

If they have a popular thought they have to go into a darkened room and lie down until it passes.

I think the point at which we fell out was when he said, 'I think,' and I said, 'I don't give a fuck what you think.'
Kelvin Mackenzie, English tabloid newspaper editor

I taught an effective writing seminar where I would go and there would be a group of business people and I would try to get them not to write 'Enclosed please find the enclosed enclosure.'
Dave Barry, *Miami Herald* columnist

Tony Grieg: Nobody's ever made a century here without learning a bit about the Aussie vernacular.
Ian Healy: What part of the body is that?
Channel Nine cricket commentary, 2005 Boxing Day Test

If you didn't want Kerry to read something, you wrote a memo longer than one page.
Trevor Sykes, former Packer employee, following Kerry Packer's death in December 2005

It takes a lot of years to make hammers out of words, but they're not profane words. They're just plain words arranged properly.
Paul Keating, Australian prime minister

I love deadlines. I like the whooshing sound they make as they fly by.
Douglas Adams (1952-2001), British writer

He has occasional flashes of silence that make his conversation perfectly delightful.
Sydney Smith (1771-1845), English writer and clergyman

The trouble with her is that she lacks the power of conversation but not the power of speech.

England and America are two countries divided by a common language.

The greatest problem of communication is the illusion that it has been accomplished.
George Bernard Shaw (1856-1950), Irish playwright and Nobel Prize winner

A fanatic is one who can't change his mind and won't change the subject.

This report, by its very length, defends itself against the risk of being read.
Winston Churchill (1874-1965), British prime minister

A memorandum is written not to inform the reader but to protect the writer.
Dean Acheson (1893-1971), American secretary of state

Talk to people about themselves and they will listen for hours.
Benjamin Disraeli (1804-81), British politician and writer

Man does not live by words alone, despite the fact that sometimes he has to eat them.
Adlai Stevenson (1900-65), American politician and diplomat

You can pick out the actors by the glazed look that comes into their eyes when the conversation wanders away from themselves.
Michael Wilding (1912-79), British actor and director

The freelance writer is a man who is paid per piece, or per word, or perhaps.
Robert Benchley (1889-1945), American writer and member of the Round Table

The most beautiful words in the English language are 'cheque enclosed'.

There's a helluva distance between wisecracking and wit. Wit has truth in it; wisecracking is simply callisthenics with words.

Don't look at me in that tone of voice.
Dorothy Parker (1893-1967), American writer and member of the Round Table

The trouble with talking too fast is you may say something you haven't thought of yet.
Ann Landers (1918-2002), American agony aunt

A friend described my voice as being like the opening of a coffin.
Quentin Crisp (1908-99), English-born writer and gay icon

He speaks to me as if I were a public meeting.
Queen Victoria (1819-1901), British monarch, about William Gladstone, British prime minister

When your work speaks for itself, don't interrupt.
Henry J Kaiser (1882-1967), American industrialist

Beware of the conversationalist who adds 'in other words'. He is merely starting afresh.
Robert Morley (1908-92), British actor

Author: Should I put more fire in my stories?
Maugham: No. Vice versa.
An aspiring author asking Somerset Maugham for advice

Culture and Media

In Australia we've got culture up to our freckles.
Les Patterson, a Barry Humphries' character

Literature is most about having sex and not much about having children. Life is the other way round.
David Lodge, British writer, *The British Museum is Falling Down*

William Shakespeare wrote for the masses. If he were alive today, he'd probably be the chief scriptwriter on *All in the Family* or *Dallas*.
Rupert Murdoch, Australian-born businessman

I don't watch television, I think it destroys the art of talking about oneself.
Stephen Fry, English writer and actor

Television enables you to be entertained in your home by people you wouldn't have in your home.
David Frost, British chat-show host

McCartney: Will there be another Royal Jubilee Concert?
Queen: Not in my garden.
Paul McCartney and Queen Elizabeth II following a pop concert in Buckingham Palace garden

So you spend your whole year with your head in a book or with a book in your head.
Simon Balderstone, Australian writer and consultant, to a best-selling Australian author after hearing how the author divides his year (reading or writing)

Some sad news—NBC has canceled *The West Wing*. That's when you know things are bad, when even fictional Democrats aren't doing well. Can't even get elected on TV anymore.
Jay Leno, American chat-show host

If parliament wasn't sitting in Canberra, it was sitting for Clifton Pugh.

Adams' first law of television: the weight of the backside is greater than the force of the intellect.
Phillip Adams, Australian writer and broadcaster, about the artist's frequent work on portraits of politicians

The shelf life of the modern hardback writer is somewhere between the milk and the yoghurt.
John Mortimer, English writer and barrister

Don't you wish there was a knob on the TV to turn up the intelligence? There's one marked 'brightness' but it doesn't work.
Eugene Gallagher

Disraeli: Thank you for the manuscript. I shall lose no time in reading it.
Benjamin Disraeli's response to an aspiring author who sent him a manuscript and asked for his opinion.

As a work of art it reminds me of a long conversation between two drunks.
Clive James, Australian-born writer and critic, about a new Judith Kransky book

I took a speed-reading course and read *War and Peace* in twenty minutes. It involves Russia.
Woody Allen, American comedian

Definition of a classic: a book everyone is assumed to have read and often thinks they have.
Alan Bennett, British author and playwright

If he has done nothing else for American culture, he has given it two of the great lies of the twentieth century: 'I buy it for the fiction' and 'I buy it for the interview'.
Nora Ephron, American writer and film producer, about *Playboy* magazine

In Russia we only had two TV channels. Channel One was propaganda. Channel Two consisted of a KGB officer telling you: Turn back at once to Channel One.

Yakov Smirnoff, Russian-born comedian, who lives in America and is popular with Republican presidents

If you read a lot of books, you're said to be well-read, but if you watch a lot of television you're not said to be 'well-viewed'.

Lily Tomlin, American comedian

What is missing in the theatre today? What is missing in the theatre today more than anything else, I think, is Vitamin E. That's Vitamin E for Edna.

Dame Edna Everage, Australian housewife superstar

Attlee: Feeling a bit standoffish today, Winston?
Churchill: That's right, Clement. Every time you see something big, you want to nationalise it.

Clement Attlee and Winston Churchill, in a male toilet when Churchill chose to use a urinal on the opposite wall to Attlee.

A bookstore is one of the only pieces of evidence we have that people are still thinking.

The big advantage of a book is it's very easy to rewind. Close it and you're right back at the beginning.

Jerry Seinfeld, American comedian

I was busy with war and torture. When you're worried about the Bushes—two generations of them—you never get to write about sex.

Maureen Dowd, *New York Times* columnist, in an interview about her book *Are Men Necessary?*

A critic is a man who knows the way but can't drive the car.
Kenneth Tynan (1927-80), British critic

My dear anonymous letter writers, if you think it so easy to be a critic, so difficult to be a poet or a painter, may I suggest you try both? You may discover why there are so few critics, and so many poets.
Pauline Kael (1919-2001), American film critic

Has anybody ever seen a drama critic in the daytime? Of course not. They come out after dark, up to no good.
P G Wodehouse (1881-1975), English-born writer

Reporter: What effect on history do you think it would have made if, in 1963, President Khrushchev had been assassinated instead of President Kennedy?
Vidal: With history one can never be certain, but I think I can safely say that Aristotle Onassis would not have married Mrs Khrushchev.
Gore Vidal (also attributed to Mikhail Gorbachev)

The only 'ism' Hollywood believes in is plagiarism.

His ignorance was an Empire State Building of ignorance. You had to admire it for its size.
Dorothy Parker about Harold Ross, founding editor of the *New Yorker* and fellow Round Table member

All music is folk music, I ain't ever heard no horse sing a song.
Louis Armstrong (1901-71), American singer and musician

A man of many talents—all of them minor.
Leslie Halliwell (1929-89), British film historian, about Blake Edwards, American film director

A classic is a book that everybody wants to have read and nobody wants to read.
Mark Twain (1835-1910), American writer

I read him for the first time in the early forties, something about bells, balls and bulls, and loathed it.
Vladimir Nabakov (1899-1977), Russian-born writer, about Ernest Hemingway

A leader in public thought in Hollywood wouldn't have sufficient mental acumen anywhere else to hold down a place in the bread line.
Anita Loos (1889-1991), American screenwriter whose work includes *Gentlemen Prefer Blondes*

I thought *Deep Throat* was a movie about a giraffe.
Bob Hope (1903-2003), American comedian and actor

Friend: Marc, your head feels as smooth as my wife's ass.
Connelly: So it does, so it does.
Marc Connelly, Round Table member, to fellow Round Table member who had patted Connelly's head when he arrived at the table.

Ads are the cave art of the twentieth century.
Marshall McLuhan (1911-1980), Canadian academic and philosopher

That isn't writing at all—it's typing.
Truman Capote (1924-84), American writer, about Beat writers including Jack Kerouac

I read the newspapers avidly. It is my one form of continuous fiction.
Aneurin Bevan (1897-1960), Welsh politician and member of WWII war cabinet

Newspapers should have no friends.
Joseph Pulitzer (1847-1911), American newspaper editor

A product of the untalented, sold by the unprincipled to the utterly bewildered.
Al Capp (1907-79), American cartoonist about newspapers

The mama of Dada.
Clifton Fadiman (1904-99), American critic, about feminist writer Gertrude Stein

Hemingway's remarks are not literature.
Gertrude Stein (1874-1946), American writer and feminist

Opera is when a guy gets stabbed in the back and, instead of bleeding, he sings.
Ed Gardner (1901-63), American comedian

Architecture is the art of how to waste space.
Philip Johnson (1906-2005), American architect

Wagner's music is better than it sounds.
Mark Twain (1835-1910), American writer

If it weren't for Philo T Farnsworth, inventor of television, we'd still be eating frozen radio dinners.
Johnny Carson (1925-2005), American chat-show host

I find television very educating. Every time somebody turns on the set, I go into the other room and read a book.
Groucho Marx (1890-1977), American comedian

Lady Astor: If I were your wife, I'd poison your coffee.
Churchill: If I were your husband, I'd drink it.
An exchange between Lady Nancy Astor and Winston Churchill

Dear boy, why not try acting?
Laurence Olivier (1907-1989), English actor, to Dustin Hoffman during the filming of *Marathon Man* when Hoffman was struggling with his role

Death and Taxes

My husband, Norm, is no longer with us. I often go to the cemetery and buff up his obelisk.
Dame Edna Everage, Australian housewife superstar

Good career move.
Gore Vidal, American writer, about the death of writer Truman Capote

I told the Inland Revenue I didn't owe them a penny because I lived near the seaside.
Ken Dodd, English comedian

There is one difference between a tax collector and a taxidermist: the taxidermist leaves the hide.
Mortimer Caplin, US Internal Revenue Service commissioner in 1963

When I die, I'm going to leave my body to science fiction.
Steven Wright, American actor, writer and comedian

The difference between tax avoidance and tax evasion is the thickness of a prison wall.
Denis Healey, British Labour politician

Child: How did you become a war hero?
JFK: It was involuntary. They sank my boat.
John F Kennedy on the circumstances of his 'war hero' status

I hold in my hand 1,379 pages of tax simplification.
Delbert L Latta, US congressman

People shouldn't worry about Asian bird flu, the real danger is from fried chicken.
A caller to ABC local radio 702, commenting on the increasing obesity of Australians and its impact on health, September 2005

I've been to the other side and let me tell you, son, there was nothing there.
Kerry Packer (1937-2005), Australian businessman, about his near death experience in 1990

If you die in an elevator, be sure to push the UP button.
Sam Levenson (1911-80), American writer and humorist

For Catholics, death is a promotion.
Bob Fosse (1927-87), American choreographer

I told my wife I wanted to be cremated. She's planning a barbecue.
Rodney Dangerfield (1921-2004), American comedian and actor

Memorial services are the cocktail parties of the geriatric set.
John Gielgud (1904-2000), English actor

Any man who has $10,000 left when he dies is a failure.
Errol Flynn (1909-59), Australian-born actor

How do they know?
Dorothy Parker (1893-1967), American writer, following the death of Calvin Coolidge (also attributed to Alva Johnston, US journalist)

Bing doesn't pay income tax. He just calls the government and says, 'How much do you boys need?'
Bob Hope (1903-2003), American comedian and actor, about Bing Crosby

I would like to live in Manchester, England. The transition between Manchester and death would be unnoticeable.
Mark Twain (1835-1910), American writer

Switzerland is the land of peace, understanding, milk chocolate and all those lovely snow-capped tax benefits.
David Niven (1910-83), British actor

As someone who at best can claim to be having only 'near-life' experiences these days, I'm available anytime that Death knocks on my door.

Sara Lee kills more people than unsafe sex.
Quentin Crisp (1908-99), English-born writer and gay icon

Some rob you with a six-gun and some with a fountain pen.
Woody Guthrie (1912-67), American folk singer

> **Bernard:** Of course, in the service, CMG stands for Call Me God. And KCMG for Kindly Call Me God.
> **Hacker:** What does GCMG stand for?
> **Bernard:** God Calls Me God.
> *Yes Minister* (Coined in the 1960s by English journalist, Anthony Sampson, but the delivery in this show gives it a perfect context)

Diplomats and Foreign Affairs

I've done more for Australia's foreign relations than a thousand Alexander Downers.

Dame Edna Everage, Australian housewife superstar, when she was named a 2006 Australian Legend

A diplomat is a person who can tell you to go to hell in such a way that you actually look forward to the trip.

Caskie Stinnett, American writer

Whatever it is that the government does, sensible Americans would prefer that the government do it to somebody else. This is the idea behind foreign policy.

The French are the masters of 'the dog ate my homework' school of diplomatic relations.

P J O'Rourke, American writer

Hacker: Who knows Foreign Office secrets apart from the Foreign Office?
Bernard: Only the Kremlin.
Yes Minister

There are Russian spies here now. And if we're lucky, they'll steal some of our secrets and they'll be two years behind.

Mort Sahl, American comedian

My dog Millie knows more about foreign policy than those two bozos.
George Bush Snr, American president, about Bill Clinton and Al Gore

You must be the only ambassador in the world to own a horse named after his country's foreign policy.
David Lange (1942-2005), New Zealand prime minister, about an American ambassador's racehorse named 'Lacka Reason'

Diplomacy: lying in state.
Oliver Herford (1864-1935), American writer

Diplomacy is the art of saying 'Nice doggie' until you can find a rock.
Will Rogers (1879-1935), American entertainer

An appeaser is one who feeds a crocodile, hoping it will eat him last.
Winston Churchill (1874-1965), British prime minister

Protocol, alcohol and Geritol.
Adlai Stevenson (1900-65), American politician and diplomat (Geritol is a tonic for low energy)

A diplomat these days is nothing but a head-waiter who's allowed to sit down occasionally.
James Thurber (1894-1961), American playwright, from *Romanoff and Juliet*

It's better to send middle-aged men abroad to bore each other than send young men abroad to kill each other.
Robin Cook (1946-2005), UK foreign minister, about UN negotiations with Saddam Hussein in 1998

Diplomacy without arms is like music without instruments.
Frederick the Great (1712-86), Prussian king

Eating and Drinking

My favorite animal is steak.
Fran Lebowitz, American writer

You think the French were lucky with foot and mouth, you're wrong. They didn't get it—they ate it. Probably had lovely sauce designed for it.
Eddy Monsoon, *Absolutely Fabulous*

Any dish that tastes good with capers in it, tastes even better with capers not in it.
Nora Ephron, American writer and film producer

Capote: Just look at that woman. She's practically a skeleton.
Friend: Truman, that's Anorexia Nervosa.
Capote: Darling, you know everyone.
Truman Capote and friend

I will not eat oysters. I want my food dead—not sick, not wounded—dead.
Woody Allen, American comedian and actor

Why does Sea World have a seafood restaurant? I'm halfway through my fishburger and I realise, Oh my God I could be eating a slow learner.
Lynda Montgomery

Let's get out of these wet clothes and into a dry martini.
Robert Benchley (1889-1945), American writer and member of the Round Table

A yuppie is someone who believes it's courageous to eat in a restaurant that hasn't been reviewed yet.
Mort Sahl, American comedian

Japanese is the thing, darling—everything with a pulse is dinner.

The last mosquito that bit me had to book into the Betty Ford Clinic.
Patsy Stone, ageing model from *Absolutely Fabulous*

The cane toad of coffee shops.
An Australian living in New York quoted in a newspaper about the proliferation of Starbucks coffee shops

They just opened a Starbucks in my living room.
Janeane Garafalo, American comedian and actor

They just opened a Starbucks in my pants.
George Carlin, American comedian and actor

She's a gourmet cook who can make anything. I bet she has a recipe for cold fusion.

Electricity is actually made up of extremely tiny particles called electrons, that you cannot see with the naked eye unless you have been drinking.

Without question, the greatest invention in the history of mankind is beer. Oh, I grant you that the wheel was also a fine invention, but the wheel does not go nearly as well with pizza.
Dave Barry, *Miami Herald* columnist

I have a rare intolerance to herbs which means I can only drink fermented liquids such as gin.
Julie Walters, British actor

> *Eddy:* You've given up drinking before.
> *Patsy:* Worst eight hours of my life.
> *Absolutely Fabulous*

Booze is the answer. I don't remember the question.
Denis Leary, American comedian and actor

I couldn't eat toast for years when I was drinking heavily, because it was too noisy.
Clarissa Dickson-Wright, one half of the English television chefs, *Two Fat Ladies*

Restaurants that wine, dine and dance are likely to disappoint on all counts.
David Dale, *Sydney Morning Herald* columnist

Avoid fruit and nuts. You are what you eat.
Jim Davis, American cartoonist

Life is uncertain. Eat dessert first.
Ernestine Ulmer, American writer

A hamburger is not the same thing as a car. The Bush Administration wants to reclassify fast-food jobs as manufacturing jobs. Talk about parsing the language … A quarter pounder may spend a week in your colon, but that doesn't make it a 'durable good'.
Bill Maher, American comedian

It's not a Greek restaurant!
A café owner to a waiter who dropped a pile of plates, overheard at a café on Queensland's Sunshine Coast

Sober, he was a lovely bloke and a fine newspaperman. Drunk, he was a lunatic who could pick a fight with a lamp post.
Mike Carlton, Australian journalist and radio broadcaster, about a former newspaper editor

---

Marge: Say grace, Bart.
Bart: Dear God, we paid for all this food ourselves, so thanks for nothing.
The Simpsons

I own more cattle than anyone else in the world. I own more land than any man in Australia. Why can't I get a decent fucking steak in my own house?

Kerry Packer (1937-2005), Australian businessman, at a dinner party at his home

The second day of a diet is always easier than the first. By the second day you're off it.

Jackie Gleason (1916-87), American comedian and actor

Ernie: Why don't you wash your face. I can see what you had for breakfast this morning.
Eric: Oh yeah, what did I have?
Ernie: Bacon, eggs and tomato sauce.
Eric: Wrong! That was yesterday.
Morecambe and Wise

Part of the secret of success in life is to eat what you like and let the food fight it out inside.

Training is everything. The peach was once a bitter almond; cauliflower is nothing but cabbage with a college education.

Mark Twain (1835-1910), American writer

A gourmet who thinks of calories is like a tart who looks at her watch.

James Beard (1903-1985), American chef and food writer

What's drinking? A mere pause from thinking.

Lord Byron (1788-1824), English poet

Beer is the Danish national drink and the Danish national weakness is another beer.

Clementine Paddleford (1898-1967), British writer

One reason why I don't drink is because I wish to know when I am having a good time.

Nancy Astor (1879-1964), American-born English socialite and politician

As a child my family's menu consisted of two choices: take it or leave it.
Buddy Hackett (1924-2003), American comedian and actor

> **Brill:** Why do you drink so much?
> **Martin:** I drink to forget.
> **Brill:** That's sad.
> **Martin:** It could be a lot sadder.
> **Brill:** What could be sadder than drinking to forget?
> **Martin:** I could forget to drink.
> Marty Brill and Dean Martin.

One more drink and I'd have been under the host.
Dorothy Parker (1893-1967), American writer and member of the Round Table

Everybody should believe in something: I believe I'll have another drink.
Robert Benchley (1889-1945), American writer and member of the Round Table

Education and Experience

I went to a bookstore and asked the saleswoman where the self-help section was. She said if she told me it would defeat the purpose.
Dennis Miller, American comedian

His lack of education is more than compensated for by his keenly developed moral bankruptcy.
Woody Allen, American comedian

Headlines:

Wall St lays an egg
Variety, about the 1929 Wall Street crash

Headless Body in Topless Bar
New York Post, 1982

Why should I learn algebra? I've no intention of ever going there.
Billy Connolly, Scottish comedian and actor

The North Shore school for the chronically overindulged.
A father referring to the expensive private school on Sydney's North Shore which his children attend

I'd rather have had Mr Menzies' education than a million pounds.
Joseph Chifley (1885-1951), Australian prime minister, about Robert Menzies

A highbrow is a person educated beyond his intelligence.
Brander Matthews, (1852-1929), American writer

The only thing we learn from history is that we do not learn.
Earl Warren (1891-1974), American politician

Experience is what your get when you don't get what you wanted.
Ann Landers (1918-2002), American agony aunt

Education is a method by which one acquires a higher grade of prejudices.
Laurence J Peter (1919-90), Canadian-born academic

Human beings, who are almost unique in having the ability to learn from the experience of others, are also remarkable for their apparent disinclination to do so.
Douglas Adams (1952-2001), British writer

Experience is simply the name we give our mistakes.
Oscar Wilde (1854-1900), Irish-born writer

Goldwynisms:
When I want your opinion I will give it to you.

I can answer in two words: im-possible.
Hollywood film producer Sam Goldwyn who became famous for his confused use of English and created his own class of one-liners.

Failure and Success

Winsome, lose some.
Alan Bennett, English playwright, gives his reason for cancelling an interview with a newspaper after it described him as winsome

Luck is a matter of preparation meeting opportunity.
Oprah Winfrey, Amercian chat-show host

Sybil: Don't shout at me. I've had a difficult morning.
Basil: Oh dear. What happened? Did you get entangled in the eiderdown again? Not enough cream in your éclair? Or did you have to talk to all your friends for so long that you didn't have time to perm your ears?
Fawlty Towers

Sometimes one feels that in Australia nothing fails like success.
Dame Leonie Kramer, ABC chairwoman, about her resignation from the ABC

Sometimes I worry about being a success in a mediocre world.
Lily Tomlin, American comedian and actor

Eighty percent of success is showing up.
Woody Allen, American comedian

I don't know the key to success, but the key to failure is to try to please everyone.
Bill Cosby, American actor and comedian

If at first you don't succeed, you're running about average.
M H Alderson

There is always time for failure.
John Mortimer, English barrister and writer

Trying is the first step toward failure.
Homer Simpson, character from The Simpsons

Some days you're a bug. Some days you're a windshield.
Price Cobb, American racing car driver

The world is divided into people who do things and people who get the credit. Try, if you can, to belong to the first class. There's far less competition.
Dwight Morrow (1873-1931), American politician

Well, it's no good crying over spilt milk. All we can do is bail up another cow.
Joseph Chifley (1885-1951), Australian prime minister

If at first you don't succeed, failure may be your style.
Quentin Crisp (1908-99), English-born writer and gay icon, who described himself as a 'retired waif' on his business card

Hepburn: I'm afraid I'm a little too tall for you, Mr Tracey.
Tracey: Don't worry about that, Miss Hepburn. I'll soon cut you down to size.
Katherine Hepburn and Spencer Tracey before their first film together.

Failure has gone to his head.

Be nice to people on your way up because you'll meet them on your way down.
Wilson Wizner (1876-1933), American screenwriter

If winning isn't important, why do they keep score.
Adolph Rupp (1901-77), American basketball coach

The toughest thing about success is that you've got to keep on being a success.
Irving Berlin (1888-1989), Russian-born American composer and lyricist

Those who tell you it's tough at the top have never been at the bottom.
Joe Harvey (1918-89), English football coach

Success is simply a matter of luck. Ask any failure.
Earl Wilson (1934-2005), American baseballer

My formula for success is rise early, work late, and strike oil.
J Paul Getty (1892-1976), American billionaire businessman

If at first you don't succeed, try, try again. Then give up. There's no use in being a damn fool about it.
W C Fields (1880-1946), American comedian and actor

If at first you don't succeed, find out if the loser gets anything.
William Lyon Phelps (1865-1943) American academic

Success consists of going from failure to failure without loss of enthusiasm.
Winston Churchill (1874-1965), British prime minister

Moderation is a fatal thing. Nothing succeeds like excess.
Oscar Wilde (1854-1900), Irish-born writer

I want to be the white man's brother, not his brother-in-law.
Martin Luther King (1929-68), Civil Rights campaigner

Goldwynisms:
It's more than magnificent, it's mediocre.

We'll jump off that bridge when we come to it.
Hollywood film producer Sam Goldwyn who became famous for his confused use of English and created his own class of one-liners.

Faith and Religion

All those who believe in telekinesis, raise my hand.
Emo Philips, American comedian and actor

My church accepts all denominations—fivers, tenners, twenties.
Patrick O'Connell

Not only is there no God, but try getting a plumber on weekends.

I'm astounded by people who want to 'know' the universe when it's hard enough to find your way around Chinatown.
Woody Allen, American comedian, actor and film director

Puritanism is the haunting fear that someone, somewhere, may be happy.
H L Mencken (1880-1956), American journalist and satirist

I admire the Pope. I have a lot of respect for anyone who can tour without an album.
Rita Rudner, American comedian and writer

Why is it that when we talk to God we're said to be praying, but when God talks to us we're schizophrenic?
Lily Tomlin, American comedian and actor

There are no atheists on a turbulent aircraft.
Erica Jong, American writer

Q: Is your husband religious?
Mrs Frost: Oh, yes, he thinks he's God Almighty.
Mrs Frost about her husband, Sir David Frost

I'd rather have my arse sawn off, varnished and sold in a provincial gift shop.
Will Self, English writer, about reading photocopied family updates sent at Christmas, from *Grumpy Old Men at Christmas*

Aren't we forgetting the true meaning of Christmas? You know, the birth of Santa.
Bart Simpson, character from *The Simpsons*

Friend: What are you doing reading the Bible?
Fields: I'm looking for loopholes.
The non-religious W C Fields, to a friend, in hospital shortly before his death.

Christmas is a race to see which gives out first: your money or your feet.
Roy Price

She's definitely a Buddhist. I heard her chant for a BMW.
Birthday Girl, a British television movie

You may be sceptical, but feng shui is actually based on solid astrological principles that have been scientifically verified by Shirley MacLaine and other leading Californians.

... the principles of 'feng shui', an ancient Chinese philosophy whose name means, literally, 'new fad'.
Dave Barry, *Miami Herald* columnist

My only hope is when those terrorists get to heaven, they meet up with the kind of virgins we had in Catholic school: Sister Mike Ditka from Our Mother of Eternal Retribution.
Robin Williams, American comedian and actor

Since only 15 per cent of Americans said they believe in evolution in a recent poll, America must change its name to the United States of Jesus Christ.
Bill Maher, American comedian

I do benefits for all religions. I'd hate to blow the hereafter on a technicality.
Bob Hope (1903-2003), American comedian and actor

Faith may be defined briefly as an illogical belief in the occurrence of the improbable.
H L Mencken (1880-1956), American journalist and satirist

I love Christmas. I receive a lot of wonderful presents I can't wait to exchange.
Henny Youngman (1906-98), American comedian and violinist

George W Bush

Political pundits are saying President George W Bush has made gains in two key states: dazed and confused.

At a press conference yesterday President Bush was asked if he had seen 'Brokeback Mountain.' He said he hadn't seen the movie but is interested in drilling for oil there.
David Letterman, chat-show host

He keeps saying 'sacrifice' and the 'war on terror,' and you turn around and he's in a field of poppies with Lance Armstrong.

President Bush announced we're going to Mars, which means he's given up on Earth.
Jon Stewart, American comedy show host

Earlier today, the White House released President Bush's tax return. Not surprisingly, under dependents, the president listed Iraq.

Senator Ted Kennedy said that Iraq was President Bush's Vietnam. When he heard about it, President Bush said, 'That's not true; I went to Iraq'.
Conan O'Brien, American chat-show host

He's like the Peanuts' character Pigpen. Wherever he goes, he stirs up such a humungous mess, it can only be cleaned up by Halliburton.

I'm not impressed by what college your kid is going to. George Bush went to Yale. The End.

The president finally explained why he sat in that classroom on 9/11 for seven minutes after he was told the country was under attack. He said he was 'collecting his thoughts.' What a time to start a new hobby.

The Dalai Lama visited the White House and told the president that he could teach him to find a higher state of consciousness. Then, after talking to Bush for a few minutes, he said, 'You know what? Let's just grab lunch.'

I mean, think about it. Other than the war in Iraq, the Katrina disaster, the deficit, the CIA leak, torture, stopping stem cell research, homeland security, global warming and undercutting science, we've yet to really feel the negative effects of the Bush administration.

Some sad news; President Bush's lapdog passed away. Gee, I didn't even know Tony Blair was sick.
Jay Leno, American chat-show host

It's their reality. We just live and die in it.
Maureen Dowd, *New York Times* columnist, from her book *Bushworld*

'Vice' started his own war. Now that's a credential!
Maureen Dowd, *New York Times* columnist, about Vice President Dick Cheney in a column comparing Vice's credentials with Jack Murtha's, who had served in the marines for 37 years and was querying the Iraq war.

Habits and Addictions

A cigarette is a pipe with a fire at one end and a fool at the other.
Kurt Vonnegut, American writer

Reality is just a crutch for people who can't cope with drugs.
Robin Williams, American comedian

I tried sniffing coke once, but ice cubes went up my nose.

I'm addicted to placebos. I'd give them up, but it wouldn't make any difference.
Steven Wright, American actor, writer and comedian

I have taken more out of alcohol than alcohol has taken out of me.
Winston Churchill (1874-1965), British prime minister

Wilde: Do you mind if I smoke?
Bernhardt: I don't care if you burn.
An exchange between Oscar Wilde and Sarah Bernhardt

I was so horrified when I read about the effects of smoking that I gave up reading.

My grandmother is over eighty and still doesn't need glasses. Drinks right out of the bottle.
Henny Youngman (1906-98), American comedian and violinist

I wouldn't recommend sex, drugs, or insanity for everyone, but they've always worked for me.

Hunter S Thompson (1937-2005), American writer and creator of Gonzo journalism

If you drink, don't drive. Don't even putt.

I feel sorry for people who don't drink. Imagine waking up in the morning and knowing that's as good as they're going to feel all day.

Dean Martin (1917-1995), American singer, actor and comedian

Giving up smoking is easy. I've done it thousands of times.

Mark Twain (1835-1910), American writer

Saffy: I thought they didn't let people with drug convictions into America.
Patsy: It's not so much a conviction, darling. It's more of a strong belief.

Absolutely Fabulous

Henry Kissinger

There cannot be a crisis next week, my schedule is full.

University politics are vicious precisely because the stakes are so small.

Power is the great aphrodisiac.

I don't stand on protocol. Just call me 'your excellency'.

Now when I bore people at a party, they think it's their fault.

Ninety per cent of politicians give the other ten per cent a bad reputation.

No one will ever win the battle of the sexes; there's too much fraternizing with the enemy.

I am being frank about myself in this book. I tell of my first mistake on page 850.

Henry Kissinger may be a great writer, but anyone who finishes his book is definitely a great reader.
Walter Isaacson, American businessman and writer

Kissinger won a Nobel Prize for watching a war end that he was for.
Eugene McCarthy (1916-2005), American politician

Nixon's the kind of guy that if you were drowning 50 feet off shore, he'd throw you a 30 foot rope. Then Kissinger would go on TV the next night and say that the President had met you more than half-way.
Mort Sahl, American comedian

Home and Family

When I get a lot of tension headaches, I do what it says on the aspirin bottle: take two and keep away from children.

When my husband comes home, if the kids are still alive, I figure I've done my job.
Roseanne Barr, American comedian

Lady Elizabeth: I wish I were a book, and then I should have more of your company.
Dryden: Pray my dear, if you do become a book, let it be an almanack, for then I may change you every year.
John Dryden, eighteenth century English poet, to his wife

My mother is a travel agent for all guilt trips.
Ruby Wax, American-born English comedian

A Freudian slip is when you say one thing but mean your mother.
Anon

Smoke can't get in there, otherwise you would have looked like prosciutto.
Eddy Monsoon to her daughter Saffy, when Saffy was pregnant and Patsy smoking

A mixed race baby is the finest accessory I could have.
Eddy Monsoon, *Absolutely Fabulous* on hearing that the father of Saffy's child was black

My parents used to take me to the pet department and tell me it was a zoo.
Billy Connolly, Scottish comedian and actor

A mother's place is in the wrong.
Roberta Taylor, English actress, well known for her role as Inspector Gina Gold in *The Bill*

Cleaning your house while your kids are still growing is like shovelling the walk before it stops snowing.
Phyllis Diller, American comedian

I accept that I am at midlife, albeit in the same way that I accept collect call from my 14-year-old, ie, grudgingly.
Susan Maushart, American-born writer and columnist for the *The Australian*

Be nice to your children. After all, they are going to choose your nursing home.
Steven Wright, American actor, writer and comedian

People who say they sleep like a baby usually don't have one.
Leo J Burke

She's not back yet. I would have felt a tremor in my bank balance.
Ben Harper, character from television comedy, *My Family*, about his daughter

For many people the advantage of living in Canberra is that their relatives are interstate.
Alan Fitzgerald, Australian journalist

My husband and I are either going to buy a dog or have a child. We can't decide whether to ruin our carpet or ruin our lives.
Rita Rudner, American comedian

'Let's take the baby to a restaurant!' Now, to a normal, sane person, this statement is absurd. It's like saying: 'Let's take a moose to the opera!'
Dave Barry, *Miami Herald* columnist

Adolescence is the stage between puberty and adultery.
Dennis Norden, English comedian

Never raise your hands to your kids. It leaves your groin unprotected.

Red Buttons, American comedian and actor

When I was a boy of 14, my father was so ignorant I could hardly stand to have the old man around. But when I got to be 21, I was astonished at how much the old man had learned in seven years.

Mark Twain (1835-1910), American writer

B J: You married?
Hawkeye: Someone's going to have to get me pregnant first.
M*A*S*H

When I was a kid, my parents moved a lot. But I always found them.

Rodney Dangerfield (1921-2004), American comedian and actor

Guilt: the gift that keeps on giving.

I never ironed my husband's pajamas. And if I raised my hand to wipe the hair out of my children's eyes, they'd flinch and call their attorney.

I'm trying very hard to understand this generation. They have adjusted the timetable for childbearing so that menopause and teaching a sixteen-year-old how to drive a car will occur in the same week.

Erma Bombeck (1927-96), American writer

My next door neighbor just had a pacemaker installed. They're still working the bugs out, though. Every time he makes love, my garage door opens.

Bob Hope (1903-2003), American comedian and actor

Every dog should have a few fleas; keeps him from worrying so much about being a dog.

Familiarity breeds contempt ... and children.
Mark Twain (1835-1910), American writer

It's a recession when your neighbour loses his job; it's a depression when you lose yours.
Harry Truman (1884-1972), American president

There was no need to do any housework at all. After the first four years the dirt doesn't get any worse.
Quentin Crisp (1908-99), English-born writer and gay icon

After two days in hospital, I took a turn for the nurse.
W C Fields (1880-1946), American comedian and actor

Insults

The 'g' is silent—the only thing about her that is.
Julie Burchill, English journalist, about Camille Paglia

Look, there's thick George, he's got a brain the size of a weasel's wedding tackle.
Blackadder, in *Blackadder III*

He has left his body to science—and science is contesting the will.
David Frost, English chat-show host

The difference between Rush Limbaugh and The Hindenburg is that one is a flaming Nazi gasbag, and one was a dirigible.
Doonesbury cartoon

Female voter: Mr Churchill, I approve of neither your politics nor your moustache.
Churchill: Do not worry, madam, you are unlikely to come in contact with either.
Winston Churchill grew a moustache in his twenties in an attempt to look older.

He looks like a brown condom stuffed with walnuts.
Clive James, Australian-born writer, about Arnold Schwarzenegger

When Ronald Reagan got Alzheimer's, how could they tell?
George Carlin, American comedian and actor

Marilyn Monroe is good at playing abstract confusion in the same way that a midget is good at being short.
Clive James, Australian-born writer

Like being savaged by a dead sheep.

Denis Healey, British Labour politican, about Geoffrey Howe, a political opponent

> **Guest:** Is there anywhere they do French food?
> **Basil:** Yes, France, I believe. They seem to like it there. And the swim would certainly sharpen your appetite. You'd better hurry, the tide leaves in six minutes.
> *Fawlty Towers*

Boy George is all England needs—another queen who can't dress.

Joan Rivers, American comedian

He has a heart like a twelve-minute egg.

Jay McInerney, American writer

You wouldn't get away with that if my scriptwriter was here.

Bob Hope (1903-2003), American comedian and actor

I've had a wonderful evening—but this wasn't it.

I've a good mind to join a club and beat you over the head with it.

Groucho Marx (1890-1977), American comedian and actor

A pile of shit in silk stocking.

Napoleon Bonaparte (1769-1821), French emporer, about Charles-Maurice de Talleyrand

You get the feeling that Dan Quayle's golf bag doesn't have a full set of irons?

Chevy Chase couldn't ad-lib a fart after a baked-bean dinner.

Johnny Carson (1925-2005), American chat-show host

He looked at me as if I were a side dish he hadn't ordered.

Ring Lardner (1885-1933), American sportswriter

The great thing about Errol was that you knew precisely where you were with him—because he always let you down.
David Niven (1910-83), British actor, about Errol Flynn

Sybil: Do you really imagine, even in your wildest dreams, that a girl like this could possibly be interested in an ageing brilliantined stick insect like you?
Sybil Fawlty to Basil in Fawlty Towers

Sir Stafford has a brilliant mind until it is made up.
Lady Violet Bonham-Carter (1887-1969), British politician, about Sir Stafford Cripps

The only flair is in her nostrils.
Pauline Kael (1919-2001), American film critic

...you rancorous coiffured old sow. Why don't you syringe the doughnuts out of your ears and get some sense into that dormant organ you keep hidden in that rat's maze of yours?
Basil Fawlty to Sybil

She turned down the role of Helen Keller because she couldn't remember the lines.
Joan Rivers, American comedian

If he were any dumber, he'd be a tree.
Barry Goldwater, American politician, about William Scott, also a politician

Any fool can criticise—and many of them do.
Cyril Garbett, British writer

The difference between genius and stupidity is that genius has its limits
Albert Einstein (1879-1955), German-born physicist and Nobel Prize winner

You had to stand in line to hate him.
Hedda Hopper (1885-1966), Hollywood gossip columnist, about Harry Cohn, US film producer

Reader, suppose you were an idiot; and suppose you were a member of Congress; but I repeat myself.
Mark Twain (1835-1910), American writer

He couldn't lead a flock of homing pigeons.
Billy Hughes (1864-1952), Australian prime minister, about Sir Robert Menzies

He was not only a bore, he bored for England.
Malcolm Muggeridge (1903-90), British journalist, about Anthony Eden

She's got brains enough for two, which is the exact quantity the girl who marries you will need.
P G Wodehouse (1881-1975), British-born writer

He occasionally stumbled over the truth, but hastily picked himself up and hurried on as if nothing had happened.

They are not fit to manage a whelk stall.

A smile like a Siberian winter.

He has all of the virtues I dislike and none of the vices I admire.
Winston Churchill (1874-1965), British prime minister

I doubt even the premier's ability to handle the petty cash box at a hot-dog stand at the local Sunday school picnic.
George Moss, Australian politician about Henry Bolte, Victorian premier

Journalism

Investigative reporting is not stenography.
Maureen Dowd, *New York Times* columnist, on the failure of a colleague to query information leaked by Bush White House sources

...we have a newspaper called *The New York Times*, which is something like *Pravda* was under the Soviet Union.
Gore Vidal, American writer and satirist

Being a reporter is as much a diagnosis as a job description.
Anna Quindlen, American journalist

I've always said there's a place for the press but they haven't dug it yet.
Tommy Docherty, Scottish football coach

It's amazing that the amount of news that happens in the world every day always just exactly fits the newspaper.
Jerry Seinfeld, American comedian

Exclusives aren't what they used to be. We tend to put 'exclusive' on everything just to annoy other papers. I once put 'exclusive' on the weather by mistake.
Piers Morgan, English newspaper editor

All of us learn to write by the second grade, then most of us go on to other things.
Bobby Knight, American basketball coach, about reporters

A foreign correspondent is someone who flies around from hotel to hotel and thinks the most interesting thing about any story is the fact that he has arrived to cover it.
Tom Stoppard, British playwright

I like *The Times*. It's not too rough on the buttocks.
Owen Newitt, character from television comedy, *The Vicar of Dibley*

I do not mean to be the slightest bit critical of TV newspeople, who do a superb job, considering that they operate under severe time constraints and have the intellectual depth of hamsters. But TV news can only present the 'bare bones' of a story; it takes a newspaper, with its capability to present vast amounts of information, to render the story truly boring.

Dave Barry, *Miami Herald* columnist

The American mass media have achieved what American political might could not: world domination.

Akbar S Ahmed, Pakistani-born academic

Headlines:
Stick it up your junta!
The Sun, British boycott of Argentine beef during Falklands conflict, 1982
Up yours, Delors
The Sun, 1990, to Jacques Delors EC president

Television has a real problem. They have no page two. Consequently every big story gets the same play and comes across to the viewer as a really big, scary one.

Art Buchwald, American newspaper columnist

Journalists do not live by words alone, although sometimes they have to eat them.

Adlai Stevenson (1900-65), American politician and diplomat

Literature is the art of writing something that will be read twice; journalism what will be grasped at once.

Cyril Connolly (1903-74), English writer

Get your facts first, and then you can distort 'em as much as you please.

Mark Twain (1835-1910), American writer

There is much to be said in favour of modern journalism. By giving us the opinions of the uneducated, it keeps us in touch with the ignorance of the community.
Oscar Wilde (1854-1900), Irish-born writer

Journalism is literature in a hurry.
Matthew Arnold (1822-88), English poet

Newspapers are unable, seemingly, to discriminate between a bicycle accident and the collapse of civilisation.
George Bernard Shaw (1856-1950), Irish playwright and Nobel Prize winner

If one morning I walked on top of the water across the Potomac River, the headline that afternoon would read: 'President Can't Swim.'
Lyndon B Johnson (1908-73), American president

Trying to determine what is going on in the world by reading newspapers is like trying to tell the time by watching the second hand of a clock.
Ben Hecht (1894-1964), American screenwriter

A good newspaper, I suppose, is a nation talking to itself.
Arthur Miller (1915-2005), American playwright

Journalism largely consists of saying 'Lord Jones is dead' to people who never knew Lord Jones was alive.
G K Chesterton (1874-1936), English writer

Facing the press is more difficult than bathing a leper.
Mother Teresa (1910-97), Albanian-born Catholic nun

In a spider web of facts, many a truth is strangled.
Paul Eldridge (1888-1982), American writer

Egghead weds hourglass
Variety headline, about Arthur Miller's marriage to Marilyn Monroe
Close but no cigar
Headline on the US Senate vote not to prosecute Bill Clinton; *New York News*, 1999

Love, Sex and Marriage

If love is the answer, could you rephrase the question.
Lily Tomlin, American actress and comedian

According to a new survey, women say they feel more comfortable undressing in front of men than they do undressing in front of other women. They say that women are too judgmental, where, of course, men are just grateful.
Jay Leno, American chat-show host

I thought *coq au vin* was love in a lorry.
Victoria Wood, British comedian

Condoms aren't completely safe. A friend of mine was wearing one and got hit by a bus.
Bob Rubin

Before I met my husband, I'd never fallen in love, though I'd stepped in it a few times.

When I finally met Mr Right, I had no idea his first name was 'Always'.

When I meet a man I ask myself, 'Is this the man I want my children to spend their weekends with?'
Rita Rudner, American comedian

Mae West
When I'm good, I'm very good, but when I'm bad, I'm better.
A man in the house is worth two in the street.
It's not the men in your life that matters, it's the life in your men.

A guy knows he's in love when he loses interest in his car for a couple of days.
Tim Allen, American actor

A man does not have to be a bigamist to have one wife too many.
The Farmer's Almanac 1966

A quick word about oral contraception; I asked a woman to sleep with me and she said 'no.'
Woody Allen, American comedian

Wedding ceremonies should only be performed at Lourdes, because it obviously takes a miracle to make a marriage work.
Kathy Lette, Australian-born author, *Dead Sexy*

Mae West
Between two evils, I always pick the one I never tried before.

I used to be Snow White, but I drifted.

Never marry for money. Divorce for money.
Wendy Liebman, American comedian

You can't bring logic into this. We're talking about Marriage. Marriage is like the Middle East. There's no solution.
Shirley, from *Shirley Valentine*

My wife and I were happy for twenty years. Then we met.

My wife and I keep fighting about sex and money. I think she charges me too much.

When my wife has sex with me, there's always a reason. One night she used me to time an egg.
Rodney Dangerfield (1921-2004), comedian

He's a hard dog to keep on the porch.
Hillary Clinton about Bill Clinton

That's what 'wife' stands for isn't it? W-I-F-E...Washing-Ironing-Fucking-Etc?
Kathy Lette, Australian writer, *Dead Sexy*

If you want sex, have an affair. If you want a relationship, buy a dog.
Julie Burchill, English writer

It's been so long since I made love, I can't remember who gets tied up.
Joan Rivers, American comedian

I've been on so many blind dates, I should get a free dog.
Wendy Liebman, American comedian

Homosexuality in Russia is a crime and the punishment is seven years in prison, locked up with other men. There is a three-year waiting list.
Yakov Smirnoff, Russian comedian

I can't understand why more people aren't bisexual. It would double your chances for a date on Saturday night.
Woody Allen, American comedian

You can make a lot of money out of golf. Ask any of my ex-wives.

My grandad said the only way to forget about a woman is find another one.
Lee Trevino, American golfer

Love is the answer, but while you are waiting for the answer, sex raises some pretty good questions.
Woody Allen, American comedian

You know that look women give you when they want to have sex with you? Neither do I.
Steve Martin, American comedian

These are not grounds for impeachment. These are grounds for divorce.
Maureen Dowd, *New York Times* columnist, on President Bill Clinton's behaviour during the 'Monica Lewinsky affair'

I'm a trisexual. I'll try anything once.
Samantha Jones in *Sex and the City*

I'm a very committed wife. And I should be committed too—for being married so many times.
Elizabeth Taylor, American actress

When I was a young man the only motor vehicle emissions that took place was while having a naughty in the back seat of one.
Gough Whitlam, Australian prime minister, during a Cabinet meeting discussion about motor vehicle emissions.

Now that the kids are grown and gone, I thought it might be time for us to have sex.
A middle-aged man to his wife in a *New Yorker* cartoon

I married beneath me—all women do.
Lady Nancy Astor, English politician

Men marry because they are tired; women because they are curious. Both are disappointed.
Oscar Wilde (1854-1900), Irish-born writer

The secret to a happy marriage remains a secret.
Henny Youngman (1906-98), American comedian and violinist

It's hard for me to get used to these changing times. I can remember when the air was clean and sex was dirty.
George Burns (1896-1996), American comedian

The husband who wants a happy marriage should learn to keep his mouth shut and his checkbook open.
Groucho Marx (1890-1977), American comedian and actor

I have learned that only two things are necessary to keep one's wife happy. First, let her think she's having her own way. And second, let her have it.
Lyndon B Johnson (1908-73), American president

Why should we take advice on sex from the Pope? If he knows anything about it, he shouldn't.
George Bernard Shaw (1856-1950), Irish playwright and Nobel Prize winner

I blame my father for telling me about the birds and the bees. I was going steady with a woodpecker for two years.
Bob Hope (1903-2003), American comedian and actor

Being an old maid is like death by drowning, a really delightful sensation after you cease to struggle.
Edna Ferber (1887-1968), American writer

It serves me right for putting all my eggs in one bastard.
Dorothy Parker (1893-1967), American writer, about her abortion

Margaret Thatcher

I shan't be pulling the levers there but I shall be a very good back-seat driver.
Margaret Thatcher following her defeat as Conservative Party leader and prime minister by John Major

Reporter: Who wears the pants in your house?
Thatcher: I do. I also wash and iron them.
Dennis Thatcher, Margaret's husband

Everyone should have a Willie.
Margaret Thatcher, about Viscount Whitelaw (Willie) who she considered an indispensable member of her government

A big cat detained briefly in a poodle parlour, sharpening her claws on the velvet.
Matthew Parris, South African-born journalist and politician, about Thatcher in the House of Lords

I wouldn't say she is open-minded on the Middle East, so much as empty-headed. She probably thinks Sinai is the plural of Sinus.
Jonathan Aitken, British politician

Attila the Hen.
Clement Freud, British writer

She is the Enid Blyton of economics. Nothing must be allowed to spoil her simple plots.
Richard Holme, British journalist

I cannot bring myself to vote for a woman who has been voice-trained to speak to me as though my dog has just died.
Keith Waterhouse, English comedy writer

I am not prepared to accept the economics of a housewife.
Jacques Chirac, French president

What more does she want, this housewife? My balls on a plate?
Jacques Chirac (attributed)

I often compare Margaret Thatcher with Florence Nightingale. She stalks through the wards of our hospitals as a lady with a lamp. Unfortunately, it's a blowlamp.
Denis Healey, British chancellor of the exchequer

She has the eyes of Caligula, but the mouth of Marilyn Monroe.
Francois Mitterand (1916-96), French president

She cannot see an institution without hitting it with her handbag.
Julian Critchley (1939-2000)

The further you got from Britain, the more admired you found she was.
James Callaghan (1912-2005), English prime minister, about his successor

Men and Women

Men's magazines are more about pleasing men; women's magazines are about women pleasing men.

They used to demand equality, now they demand Botox.
Maureen Dowd, *New York Times* columnist and author of *Are Men Necessary?*, about young women's priorities

Q: What do you do if a bird craps on your windscreen?
A: Don't ask her out again.
Jim Davidson, English comedian

Men are a luxury, not a necessity.
Cher, American singer and actor

He had polyester sheets and I wanted to get cotton sheets. He discussed it with his shrink many times before he made the switch.
Mia Farrow, American actor, on Woody Allen, her former partner

Men want the same thing from their underwear that they want from women: a little bit of support, and a little bit of freedom.
Jerry Seinfeld, American comedian

God gave us all a penis and a brain, but only enough blood to run one at a time.
Robin Williams, American comedian and actor

We have reason to believe that man first walked upright to free his hands for masturbation.
Lily Tomlin, American comedian and actor

What women want: to be loved, to be listened to, to be desired, to be respected, to be needed, to be trusted, and sometimes, just to be held. What men want: tickets to the World Series.

...men and women do not have the same definition of the term 'man with a sense of humor'. To men, it means 'a man who thinks a lot of stuff is funny'. Whereas to women, it means 'a man who talks and looks kind of like Hugh Grant'.
Dave Barry, *Miami Herald* columnist

We weren't meant to have futures, we were meant to marry them.
Nora Ephron, American writer and film director

My grandmother was a tough woman. She buried three husbands and two of them were just sleeping.
Rita Rudner, American comedian

Feng shui is the ancient Chinese art of getting men to put the toilet lid down.
Jeff Green, British comedian and writer

The quickest way to a man's heart is through his chest.
Roseanne Barr, American comedian

As with most liberal sexual ideas, what makes the world a better place for men invariably makes it a duller and more dangerous place for women.
Julie Burchill, British writer

You see a lot of smart guys with dumb women, but you hardly ever see a smart woman with a dumb guy.
Erica Jong, American writer

I was born into the Jewish culture, and for all our many fine qualities, Jewish men are not known for the ability to fix things (with the exception of Arnold Rothstein, who fixed the 1919 World Series).
Gene Weingarten, Washington Post humorist

The only time a man should be put on a pedestal is when he's too short change the lightbulbs.
Kathy Lette, Australian writer, *Nip 'n' Tuck*

Every woman should have four pets in her life. A mink in her closet, a jaguar in her garage, a tiger in her bed, and a jack-ass to pay for it all.
Paris Hilton, American heiress and professional celebrity, using Mae West's original

I never married because there was no need. I have three pets at home which answer the same purpose as a husband. I have a dog which growls every morning, a parrot which swears all afternoon and a cat that comes home late at night.
Marie Corelli (1855-1924), English writer

Men get laid, but women get screwed.
Quentin Crisp (1908-99), English-born writer and gay icon

If man had created man, he would be ashamed of his performance.
Mark Twain (1835-1910), American writer

Behind every successful man is a surprised woman.
Maryon Pearson (1902-91), Canadian prime minister's wife

I sometimes think that God, in creating man, somewhat overestimated his ability.
Oscar Wilde (1854-1900), Irish-born writer

At the age of eleven or thereabouts women acquire a poise and an ability to handle difficult situations which a man, if he is lucky, manages to achieve somewhere in the later seventies.
P G Wodehouse (1881-1975), British writer

Women who seek to be equal with men lack ambition.
Timothy Leary (1920-96), American writer and counter-culture icon
Women are like elephants to me: I like to look at them, but I wouldn't want to own one.

I was in love with a beautiful blonde once. She drove me to drink; that's the one thing I'm indebted to her for.
W C Fields (1880-1946), American comedian and actor

I like to wake up each morning feeling a new man.
Jean Harlow (1911-37), American actor

Modern Life

A psychologist is selling a video that teaches you how to test your dog's IQ. Here's how it works. If you spend $12.99 on the video, your dog is smarter than you.
Jay Leno, American chat-show host

Q: What's your idea of civilisation?
Shaw: It's a good idea. Somebody ought to start it.
George Bernard Shaw (also attributed to Mahatma Gandhi)

I'm a pissed off penguin. Where are my icecaps?
Placard at a global warming demonstration, 2005

Supermarkets stand condemned as symbols of man's inhumanity to women.
Phillip Adams, Australian writer and broadcaster

Turbulence must be the best laxative known to man.

Cruises are like prisons with the possibility of drowning.
Billy Connolly, Scottish comedian, about anxiety during air travel

If high heels were so wonderful, men would still be wearing them.
Sue Grafton, English writer

I went to a general store. They wouldn't let me buy anything specific.

Right now I'm having amnesia and *deja vu* at the same time. I think I've forgotten this before.

I went to a 7-11 and asked for a 2x4 and a box of 3x5's.
Steven Wright, American actor, writer and comedian

We used to build civilisations, now we build shopping malls.
Bill Bryson, American writer

A trough of low pleasure is passing over Europe.
BBC television newsreader during a weather report

Will all the Internet billionaires go broke and be forced to use their Palm Pilots to kill rats for food?
Dave Barry, *Miami Herald* columnist

Why do they call it rush hour when nothing moves?
Robin Williams, American comedian and writer

Nice guys may appear to finish last, but usually they're running a different race.
Ken Blanchard

I think animal testing is a terrible idea; they get all nervous and give the wrong answers.
Stephen Fry and Hugh Laurie, from television program *A Bit of Fry and Laurie*

You can drop the attitude, you only work in a shop.
Eddy Monsoon, from *Absolutely Fabulous*

Sorry, but my karma just ran over your dogma.
Anon

You only live once. But if you work it right, once is enough.
Fred Allen (1894-1956), American comedian and radio broadcaster

I shot an elephant in my pajamas. How he got in my pajamas I don't know.
Groucho Marx (1890-1977), American comedian and actor

I told my doctor I broke my leg in two places. He told me to quit going to those places.
Henny Youngman (1906-98), American comedian and violinist

Money and Luck

People who say that money can't buy happiness just don't know where to shop.
Kathy Lette, Australian writer, *Nip 'n' Tuck*

It will squeeze the rich until the pips squeak.
Denis Healey, British chancellor of the exchequer

I'm so poor I can't even pay attention.
Ron Kittle, American baseballer

His wallet is more capacious than an elephant's scrotum and just as difficult to get your hands on.
Blackadder II

> **Q:** What exactly is the Internet?
> **A:** The Internet is a world-wide network of university, government, business and private computer systems.
> **Q:** Who runs it?
> **A:** A 13-year-old named Jason
> Dave Barry, *Miami Herald* columnist

Having money is rather like being a blonde. It is more fun but not vital.
Mary Quant, British fashion designer

...if you own stocks, you have the excitement of knowing that at any moment you could be wiped out by economic forces that you do not even dimly comprehend.
Dave Barry, *Miami Herald* columnist

Whoever stole it is spending less money than my wife.
Illie Nastase, Romanian tennis player, following the theft of his American Express card and his failure to report the theft to police

Some days you're the pigeon, some days you're the statue.
David Brent, character from British TV series, *The Office*

I'm very lucky. The only time I was up shit creek, I happened to have a paddle.
George Carlin, American comedian and actor

The best way to tell gold is to pass the nugget around a crowded bar, and ask them if it's gold. If it comes back, it's not gold.
Lennie Lower (1903-47), Australian writer

The buck stops with the guy who signs the cheque.
Rupert Murdoch (Variation of Harry Truman's 'The buck stops here')

My problem lies in reconciling my gross habits with my net income.
Errol Flynn (1909-59), Australian-born actor

A rich man's joke is always funny.
Heywood Broun (1888-1939), American journalist

Please find me a one-armed economist so we will not always hear 'on the other hand ...'
Herbert Hoover (1874-1964), US president

If you can actually count your money, then you are not really a rich man.

Money isn't everything, but it sure keeps you in touch with your children.

If you owe the bank $100, that's your problem. If you owe the bank $100 million, that's the bank's problem.
J Paul Getty (1892-1976), American businessman

I've been rich and I've been poor. It's better to be rich.
Gertrude Stein (1874-1946), American writer and feminist

When life hands you lemons, make whisky sours.
W C Fields (1880-1946), American comedian and actor

When I was young I thought that money was the most important thing in life; now that I am old I know that it is.
Oscar Wilde (1854-1900), Irish-born writer

Women don't love money with the pure spiritual flame that men do. They want to convert it into objects, jewellery, furs, clothing, accessories.

I remember that when I was young (if I ever was) my sister swept into the room where my mother and I were sitting and said the people next door had no money to speak of, doubtless quoting a grown-up. My mother replied, 'But money is never to speak of.'
Quentin Crisp (1908-99), English-born writer and gay icon

Eric: My wife's got a terrible memory.
Ernie: Really?
Eric: Yes, she never forgets a thing.
Morecambe and Wise

People and Places

Down there, they pop the bland tablet every morning.
Paul Keating, Australian prime minister, about Melbourne

This beach resort at Reunion is so exclusive not even the tide can get in.
Kathy Lette, Australian writer, *Dead Sexy*

Streets full of water. Please advise.
A (joke) telegram from Robert Benchley to his editor on his first trip to Venice.

In Canberra, even the mistakes are planned by the National Capital Development Commission.
Alan Fitzgerald, Australian journalist

It's an old Aboriginal word meaning 'Let's get together and have fun'. They gave us the word because they had no further need for it.
Barry Humphries, Australian-born entertainer, about Melbourne's Moomba Parade

The elite in this country get to act like they're the top dogs and we're just a bunch of fire hydrants out here.
Jim Hightower, American Texas-based politician

There are two seasons in Scotland: June and winter.
Billy Connolly, Scottish comedian and actor

You can always tell an Australian but you just can't tell them much.
Graffiti seen by Billy Connolly during his *World Tour of New Zealand*

The great thing about Glasgow is that if there's a nuclear attack it'll look exactly the same afterwards.
Billy Connolly, Scottish comedian

I'm Canadian. That's like American but without the guns.
Dave Foley, Canadian actor

In America you can always find a party. In Russia the party always finds you.
Yakov Smirnoff, Russian-born comedian

You can lead a horticulture but you can't make her think.
Dorothy Parker was challenged to use the word 'horticulture' in a sentence

The 51st state: the state of denial.
Kurt Vonnegut, American writer, in A Man without Country

Apart from cheese and tulips, the main product of Holland is advocaat, a drink made from lawyers.
Alan Coren, British writer and satirist

The English instinctively admire any man who has no talent and is modest about it.
James Agate, British theatre critic

Americans call it the Tonight Show so they can remember when it's on.
Jo Brand, English comedian

I've always wanted to see a ghost town. You couldn't even get a parachute to open here after 10pm.
Max Bygraves, singer, about Melbourne in 1965

A Sydney socialite.
Barry Humphries' definition of the word oxymoron, at a 1983 press conference

Look at Patty Hearst. Those parents of hers cutting those peanut butter sandwiches day after day just to turn her into an urban guerrilla.
Sandy Stone, a Barry Humphries' character

Americans don't really understand what's going on in Bosnia. To them it's the unspellables killing the unpronouncables.
P J O'Rourke, American writer

When it's three o'clock in New York, it's still 1938 in London.
Bette Midler, American singer and actor

I think Iraq and Iran should be combined into one country called Irate. All the pissed-off people live in one place and get it over with.
Denis Leary, American comedian and actor

Scottish Americans tell you that if you want to identify tartans, it's easy. You look under the kilt, and if it's a quarter-pounder, it's a McDonald's.
Billy Connolly, Scottish comedian

If Mark Twain dying in poverty in London send 500 words. If Mark Twain has died in poverty send 1000 words.
A telegram from *New York Journal* editor to their reporter in London, where Twain was visiting.

I can confirm that Russell Crowe does not use deodorant. I understand that in Australia it's known as animal magnetism.
Joan Rivers, American comedian

Thus the metric system did not really catch on in the States, unless you count the increasing popularity of the nine-millimeter bullet.
Dave Barry, *Miami Herald* columnist

Abroad is unutterably bloody and foreigners are fiends.
Uncle Matthew, a character from Nancy Mitford's *The Pursuit of Love*

Australians are just British people who are happy.
Craig Hill, Scottish comedian

We don't want to see the kangaroo taken out of Qantas.
Kim Beazley, Labor opposition leader, about the possibility of thousands of Qantas jobs being sent offshore, October 2005

Americans will put up with anything provided it doesn't block traffic.
Dan Rather, American broadcaster

The reason they're giving for the divorce is that Donald has been having a long-term affair with himself.
Arsenio Hall, American comedian and chat-show host, about Donald Trump

England's not a bad country. It's just a mean, cold, ugly, divided, tired, clapped-out, post-imperial, post-industrial slag-heap covered in polystyrene hamburger cartons.
Margaret Drabble, English novelist

Every time Europe looks across the Atlantic to see the American eagle it observes only the rear end of an ostrich.
H G Wells (1866-1946), English writer

When I told the people of Northern Ireland that I was an atheist, a woman in the audience stood up and said, 'Yes, but is it the God of the Catholics or the God of the Protestants in whom you don't believe?'
Quentin Crisp (1908-99), English-born writer and gay icon

I don't like all this fresh air. I'm from Los Angeles. I don't trust any air I can't see.
Bob Hope (1903-2003), American comedian and actor

The British tourist is always happy abroad as long as the natives are waiters.
Robert Morley (1908-92), British actor

They are like their own beer: froth on top, dregs at the bottom, the middle excellent.
Voltaire (1694-1778), French writer and philospher, about the British

Seventy-two suburbs in search of a city.
Dorothy Parker (1893-1967), American writer, about Los Angeles

Canada is useful only to provide me with furs.
Madame de Pompadour (1721-64), French courtesan, after the fall of Quebec in 1759

I've never met him, but I used to spend time in Ohio, and they turn out Gerry Fords by the bale.
Alice Roosevelt Longworth (1884-1980), daughter of President Theodore Roosevelt, about Gerald Ford

Never trust a man who combs his hair straight from his left armpit.
Alice Roosevelt Longworth, about Douglas MacArthur

America is the only nation in history which, miraculously, has gone directly from barbarism to degeneration without the usual interval of civilisation.

Americans have no capacity for abstract thought, and make bad coffee.
Georges Clemenceau (1841-1929), French prime minister

How can anyone govern a nation that has two hundred and forty-six different kinds of cheese?
Charles de Gaulle (1890-1970), French military leader and president

All Englishmen talk as if they've got a bushel of plums stuck in their throats, and then after swallowing them get constipated from the pits.
W C Fields (1880-1946), American comedian and actor

Of course, America had often been discovered before Columbus, but it had always been hushed up.
Oscar Wilde (1854-1900), Irish-born writer

Oh yes, I studied dramatics under him for twelve years.
Dwight Eisenhower (1890-1969), American president, about Douglas MacArthur

Without Britain, Europe would remain only a torso.
Ludwig Erhard (1897-1977), West German chancellor

Venice is like eating an entire box of chocolate liqueurs in one go.

It is a scientific fact that if you live in California you lose one point of your IQ every year.
Truman Capote (1924-84), American writer

Toronto is a kind of New York operated by the Swiss.
Peter Ustinov (1921-2004), British actor

It is never difficult to distinguish between a Scotsman with a grievance and a ray of sunshine.
P G Wodehouse (1881-1975), English-born writer

Hollywood is a place where they shoot too many pictures and not enough actors.
Walter Winchell 1897-1972), American journalist who conceived the gossip column

Nobody ever went broke underestimating the taste of the American public.
H L Mencken (1880-1956), American journalist and satirist

The French are a logical people, which is one reason the English dislike them so intensely. The other is that they own France, a country which we have always judged to be much too good for them.
Robert Morley (1908-92), British actor

A trip through a sewer in a glass-bottomed boat.
Wilson Wizner (1876-1933), American screenwriter, about Hollywood

Politics and Government

Just because you swallowed a fucking dictionary when you were about 15 doesn't give the right to pour a bucket of shit over the rest of us.

Paul Keating to Jim McClelland following a negative newspaper column

I guarantee if you walk into any pet shop in Australia what the resident galah will be talking about is micro-economic policy.

Whenever you put your hand in your pocket, Dr Hewson's hand will be in there too.

Paul Keating, during 1993 election campaign which had the central issue of a goods and services tax

I think he spat a silver steak knife at you, Mr Speaker.

Paul Keating in Parliament when Alexander Downer was removed from the House of Representatives chamber

At least we're doing it for the history books—you're doing if for tomorrow's fish-and-chips.

Paul Keating to a journalist

You have to make sure you are on the right tram at the right time.

Paul Keating

Why do so many people take such an instant dislike to Bronwyn Bishop? Because it saves time.

Gareth Evans, Australian foreign minister, about an ambitious Liberal senator

The ego has landed.

Frank Dobson, British politician, about Ken Livingstone, London mayoral candidate

Malcolm Fraser is the cutlery man of Australia. He was born with a silver spoon in his mouth, speaks with a forked tongue and knifes his colleagues in the back.

Bob Hawke, Australian prime minister, about his opponent in the 1983 election

Menzies: So you'll be eating some humble pie then, Fitchett?
Fitchett: Only if it's garnished with the sauce of your embarrassment.

Robert Menzies to Ian Fitchett, Canberra a legendary political journalist

Iemma is Italian for Unsworth.

James Valentine, ABC Radio announcer, on the ascension of Morris Iemma to the NSW premiership in August 2005 (Barrie Unsworth was briefly NSW premier before Labor lost power in the late 1980s)

The trouble with the joint sitting was that there was too much sitting and not enough joints.

Mungo MacCallum, Australian journalist

The first log that should be rolled is David Beddall.

Gough Whitlam, Australian prime minister, about the difficulties in 1995 of the Keating government resolving woodchip exports. Beddall was resources minister

When the honourable gentleman squawks, I never know whether it is high moon or high noon.

Gough Whitlam

Hacker: When did a civil servant last refuse an honour?
Bernard: Well I think there was somebody in the Treasury that refused a Knighthood.
Hacker: Good God. When?
Bernard: I think it was 1496.
Hacker: Why?
Bernard: He had already got one.

Yes Minister

It's called question time, not question and answer time.

Stephen Conroy, Australian politician, about the content of parliamentary question time

I think he was probably the most incontinent minister I have ever come across in terms of security. He was absolutely incapable of retaining any information longer than the time it took to bump into a journalist.

Bernard Ingham, Margaret Thatcher's press secretary, about Alan Clark, a conservative government minister

The art of politics is to get someone to change their mind without humiliating them.

Lorna Fitzsimons, British Labour politician

Poor George, he can't help it—he was born with a silver foot in his mouth.

Ann Richards, American politician, about George Bush Snr

To say that change at Westminster happens at a snail's pace is to insult the pace of snails.

Oona King, British Labour politician

Vote Labour and you build castles in the air. Vote Conservative and you can live in them.

BBC TV show, *That was the week that was*, 1962

Prudence is the other woman in Gordon's life.

Unsourced, about Gordon Brown, British chancellor of the exchequer

I am a Ford, not a Lincoln.

Gerald Ford, American president

I feel like a javelin competitor who won the toss and elected to receive.

George Bush Snr, American president

If George Bush reminds many women of their first husbands, Pat Buchanan reminds women why an increasing number of them are staying single.

Judy Pearson, American writer

Every woman's first husband.
Barbara Ehrenreich and Jane O'Reilly, about George Bush Snr

John Connally's conversion to the GOP raised the intellectual level of both parties.
Frank Mankiewicz, American journalist

Reagan won because he ran against Jimmy Carter. If he ran unopposed he would have lost.
Mort Sahl, American comedian

There's two things in the world you never want to let people see how you make 'em: laws and sausages.
Leo McGarry, character from television program, *The West Wing*

But leadership is not a series of costume changes. The former Andover cheerleader has been too reliant on photo-ops, drop-bys and 'Mission Accomplished' strut-bys, rather than a font of personal knowledge.
Maureen Dowd, *New York Times* columnist, about President George W Bush's leadership style

I don't like the thought of Dick Cheney ogling my Googling.
Maureen Dowd, about the Bush government's legal demand to Google to supply users' search information

Liberals feel unworthy of their possessions. Conservatives feel they deserve everything they've stolen.

Washington couldn't tell a lie, Nixon couldn't tell the truth, and Reagan couldn't tell the difference.
Mort Sahl, American comedian

Reagan's idea of a good farm program was *Hee Haw*.

There's nothing in the middle of the road but yellow stripes and dead armadillos.
Jim Hightower, American politician

The battle for the mind of Ronald Reagan was like the trench warfare of World War I: never have so many fought so hard for such barren terrain.
Peggy Noonan, Ronald Reagan's speechwriter

Today's public figures can no longer write their own speeches or books, and there is some evidence that they can't read them, either.
Gore Vidal, American writer

At any given moment, public opinion is a chaos of superstition, misinformation and prejudice.

Half of the American people never read a newspaper. Half never vote for President. One hopes it is the same half.

In the long run Gore is thicker than Nader.
Gore Vidal, about Al Gore, 2000 US presidential candidate (and a relative)

I am Al Gore, and I used to be the next president of the United States of America.
Al Gore, presidential candidate, after the US Supreme Court stopped counting of disputed votes in the 2000 election

You won the elections, but I won the count.
Anastasio Somoza (1925-80), Nicaraguan dictator

Mr Wilson bores me with his Fourteen Points. Why, Almighty God has only Ten Commandments!
Georges Clemenceau (1841-1929), French prime minister

Billy Snedden couldn't go two rounds with a revolving door.
Vince Gair (1902-80), Australian politician

He was never born. I think he was quarried.
Fred Daly (1913-95), Australian politician, about Billy Hughes

They couldn't, in the National Party, run a bath and if either the deputy leader or the leader tried to, Sir Robert would run away with the plug.

David Lange (1942-2005), New Zealand prime minister, about the NZ National Party (conservative) opposition

Our military forces are an arm of government, just like the Department of Social Welfare, although probably less able to inflict widespread harm.

David Lange

He's going around the country stirring up apathy.

David Lange, about opposition leader Jim Bolger (also used by in the UK by Willie Whitelaw about Harold Wilson)

Yesterday's fish and chip wrapper is today's news.

David Lange, about former fish and chip shop owner Pauline Hanson's election to the Australian parliament in 1996

Headlines from www.chaser.com.au
Striving for mediocrity in a world of excellence.
The alert that keeps you alarmed.
This site is satirical and nothing whatsoever on it is true. At all. Ever.

Comrades, this man has a nice smile, but he's got iron teeth.

Andrei Gromyko (1909-89), Soviet foreign minister, about Mikhail Gorbachev

A difficulty for every solution.

Herbert Samuel (1879-1963), British politician, about the British civil service

Throughout the year he stood like the boy on the burning deck of the Titanic, with his finger in the dyke, an apple on his head and his foot in his mouth.

Tony Banks (1943-2006), Labour minister, awarding John Major 1996 'Survivor of the Year'

When he leaves the chamber, he probably goes to vandalise a few paintings somewhere. He is to the arts what Vlad the Impaler was to origami...He is undoubtedly living proof that a pig's bladder on a stick can be elected as a Member of Parliament.

Tony Banks, about conservative MP Terry Dicks

He is simply a shiver looking for a spine to run up.

Harold Wilson (1916-95), British prime minister, about Edward Heath (also used by Paul Keating about John Hewson)

I thought he was a young man of promise; but it appears he was a young man of promises.

Arthur Balfour (1848-1930), British prime minister about Churchill

In his usual arrogant and high-handed fashion, he dons his Thatcherite jackboots and stamps all over local opinion. He is like Hitler with a beer belly.

Tony Banks (1943-2006), Labour minister, about Kenneth Clark

Morphine and state relief are the same. You go dopey, feel better and are worse off.

Martin H Fischer (1879-1962), German-born physician and author

We know what happens to people who stay in the middle of the road. They get run down.

Aneurin Bevan (1897-1960), British politician

Leaking is what you do, briefing is what I do.

James Callaghan (1912-2005), British prime minister, to a secrecy enquiry

It's the first time in recorded history that turkeys have been known to vote for an early Christmas.

James Callaghan, during a debate which resulted in the fall of his Labour Government

A sheep in sheep's clothing.

Churchill, about Clement Attlee

The best argument against democracy is a five-minute conversation with the average voter.

A merchant of discourtesy.
Winston Churchill (1874-1965), British prime minister, about Aneurin Bevan

I think a lot of gay people who are not dealing with their homosexuality get into right-wing politics.
Robert Morley (1908-92), British actor

Castro couldn't even go to the bathroom unless the Soviet Union put the nickel in the toilet.
Richard Nixon (1913-1994), US president, about Fidel Castro

He slept more than any other president, whether by day or by night.
H L Mencken (1880-1956), American journalist and satirist about Calvin Coolidge

It's a recession when your neighbour loses his job; it's a depression when you lose yours. Recovery is when Jimmy Carter loses his job.

Politics is just like show business, you have a hell of an opening, coast for a while, and then have a hell of a close.
Ronald Reagan (1911-2004), American president, California governor and Hollywood actor, in 1966

It is not enough to have every intelligent person in the country voting for me—I need a majority.
Adlai Stevenson (1900-65), American politician and diplomat

I will make a bargain with the Republicans. If they will stop telling lies about Democrats, we will stop telling the truth about them.
Adlai Stevenson (1900-65), American politician and diplomat

It's so cold I saw a politician with his hands in his own pockets.
Bob Hope (1903-2003), American comedian and actor

Gerry Ford is a nice guy, but he played too much football with his helmet off.
Lyndon B Johnson (1908-73), American president

I am against government by crony.
Harold Ickes (1874-1952), American politician

George Bush is Gerald Ford without the pizzazz.
Pat Paulsen (1927-97), American comedian

Vote for the man who promises the least; he'll be the least disappointing.
Bernard Baruch (1870-1965), American financier and political adviser

Why, this man Goldwater is living so far in the past and is so handsome that he was offered a movie contract by Eighteenth Century-Fox.
Hubert Humphrey (1911-78), American vice president, about Barry Goldwater

I don't care if you study ancient history, but don't vote for it.
Humphrey about Barry Goldwater

Don't buy a single vote more than necessary. I'll be damned if I'm going to pay for a landslide.
John F Kennedy (1917-63), American president, the text of a telegram from his father but widely attributed to JFK

Public Speaking

Hubert, a speech does not have to be eternal to be immortal.
Muriel Humphrey to her husband, Hubert and an American vice president

My father gave me these hints on speech-making: be sincere, be brief, be seated.
James Roosevelt (1907-91), son of US president Franklin D Roosevelt

An after-dinner speech should be like a lady's dress—long enough to cover the subject and short enough to be interesting.
Richard Austen Butler (1902-82), British politician

Sorry, love, cannot attend. Gielgud doesn't fielgud.
Note from John Gielgud to a friend about his inability to attend an awards function.

If you haven't struck oil in the first three minutes, stop boring.

The human brain starts working the moment you are born and never stops until you stand up to speak in public.
George Jessel (1898-1981), American entertainer, known as the 'Toastmaster General of the United States'

The head cannot take in more than the seat can endure.
Winston Churchill (1874-1965), British prime minister

The secret of a good sermon is to have a good beginning and a good ending, then having the two as close together as possible.
George Burns (1896-1996), American comedian

'In conclusion'—the phrase that wakes up the audience.
Herbert Prochnow, American banker, writer and toastmaster

I always have a quotation for every occasion—it saves original thinking.
Dorothy L Sayers (1893-1957), British writer

Aspiring politician: Mr Churchill, you heard my talk yesterday. Can you tell me how I could have put more fire into it?
Churchill: What you should have done is put it in the fire.

Always be shorter than anybody dared to hope.
Lord Reading (1860-1935), British politician

Did you ever think that making a speech on economics is a lot like pissing down your leg? It seems hot to you, but it never does to anyone else.
Lyndon B Johnson (1908-73), American president

It usually takes me more than three weeks to prepare a good impromptu speech.
Mark Twain (1835-1910), American writer

Well, I thought my razor was dull until I heard his speech.
Groucho Marx (1890-1977), American comedian and actor

Spike Milligan

One day at Spike's house
Neighbour (who knocked on front door at night): I saw you on TV last night—brilliant.
Spike: Right.
Next day
Neighbour (after being woken by Spike's knock at the door): Spike, what is it?
Spike: Saw you mowing the lawn this afternoon—brilliant.

Listen, someone's screaming in agony—fortunately I speak it fluently.

Contraceptives should be used on every conceivable occasion.

I don't mind dying. I just don't want to be there when it happens.

Is there anything worn under the kilt? No, it's all in perfect working order.

I've got Crohn's disease—and he's got mine.

Woy Woy is the only above-ground cemetery in the world.

I don't like women in positions of power because they make all the wrong bloody decisions.

Money couldn't buy friends but you got a better class of enemy.

All I ask is the chance to prove that money can't make me happy.

Anyone can be 52 but it takes a bus to be a 52A.

Her mother was a cultivated women—she was born in a greenhouse.

And God said, 'Let there be light' and there was light, but the Electricity Board said He would have to wait until Thursday to be connected.

I'd like to go there. But if Jeffrey Archer is there I want to go to Lewisham.
About the prospect of going to heaven

Then came the war. North Africa, promoted in the field (they wouldn't let me indoors). Mentioned in dispatches, nothing positive. Just mentioned.
About his army career

The RTO gave me a travel warrant, a white feather and a picture of Hitler marked 'This is your enemy'. I checked every compartment, but he wasn't on the train.
From *Adolf Hitler: My Part in His Downfall*

Spike: Why are they serving bread-and-butter pudding?
Lunch partner: Because it's Lent.
Spike: When do we have to give it back?

Bring me some soup.
A telegram to his first wife on an occasion when he was ill in bed but wasn't speaking to her

Toast please.
(Telegram to his second wife). Her reply (by telegram): On its way.

When I look back, the fondest memory I have is not really of the Goons. It is of a girl called Julia with enormous breasts.
On his 75th birthday

Little grovelling bastard.
About Prince Charles following praise from the Prince for his 1994 Lifetime Achievement Comedy award

I can't see the sense in it really. It makes me a Commander of the British Empire. They might as well make me a Commander of Milton Keynes—at least that exists.
About his honorary CBE in 1994

I suppose a knighthood is out of the question?
In a fax to Prince Charles. He was awarded an honorary KBE in 2000

Yes, but it's your mother, isn't it? You don't get board and lodging at Buckingham Palace if you don't swear an oath.
To Prince Charles who told him even he (the prince) had to swear the oath of allegiance after the comic refused to do so

He sent me a fax. It said: 'I hope you go before me because I don't want you singing at my funeral'.
Harry Secombe (1921-2001), fellow Goon

I suppose it will be my turn next to join him. But they'll have to drag me kicking and screaming.
After the death of Harry Secombe

Spike Milligan—the thinking man's idiot.
Ronnie Barker

Sport

You just dropped the World Cup.
Steve Waugh, Australian cricket captain, when South African fielder Herschelle Gibbs dropped a catch, 1999 cricket World Cup

Johnny Carson asked golfer Arnold Palmer if his wife did anything to wish him luck before a game.
Palmer: She washes my balls.
Carson: I guess that makes your putter stand up.

His googly remains as hard to read as James Joyce.
Peter Roebuck, Australian journalist, about Stuart McGill's spin bowling

Not over till the fat laddie spins.
The Sun newspaper on Shane Warne

Fishing is a jerk on one end of the line waiting for a jerk on the other end of the line.
Michael Palin, English comedian, actor and world traveller

He just couldn't quite get his leg over.
Jonathan Agnew, cricket commentator, describing Ian Botham's freak dismissal where he fell over his own stumps, 1991

Michael Kasprowicz is the master of the Rock Hudson delivery. It looks straight but it's not.
Kerry O'Keefe, ABC Radio cricket commentator

My marriages don't last this long.
John Daly, American golfer, about rain delays during a 2005 golf tournament

Although golf was originally restricted to wealthy, overweight Protestants, today it's open to anybody who owns hideous clothing.
Dave Barry, *Miami Herald* columnist

His marriage to Swedish model Elin Nordegren is now in the 'Let's watch Leno instead' stage.

Alex Kaseberg, American comedian, about Tiger Woods' marriage

Michael Holding: You know that Brian Lara actually named his first child after the ground upon which he scored his first test century, Sydney.
Bill Lawry: That's interesting.
Holding: Lucky he was not scoring the century in one of the sub-continent grounds, lets say somewhere like Lahore.

Channel Nine cricket commentary, 2005 West Indies tour

New Yorkers love it when you spill your guts out there. Spill your guts at Wimbledon and they make you stop and clean it up.

Jimmy Connors, American tennis player, about Flushing Meadow, the home of the US Open

He told me how much he enjoyed playing me, and that he hoped it happens a lot more ... and that makes one of us.

Andre Agassi, American tennis player, about Roger Federer

In Russia, if a male athlete loses, be becomes a female athlete.

Yakov Smirnoff, Russian-born comedian

I'm as rapt as a kebab with the lot.

Danny Green, a boxer, expressing his pleasure at the prospect of a fight against Anthony Mundine

Boxing's just show business with blood.

Frank Bruno, English boxer

After the match, an official asked for two players to take a dope test. I offered him the referee.

Tommy Docherty, British football coach

If you gave our strikers a 50-pound note they'd find it difficult to score in a brothel.
Tommy Docherty

I resigned as coach because of illness and fatigue. The fans were sick and tired of me.
John Ralston, American football coach

He said 'oops'. At least he said the Australian word for oops.
Dennis Cometti, AFL commentator about a player who mouthed the 'f' word on television.

It's a funny kind of month, October. For the really keen cricket fan it's when you discover that your wife left you in May.
Dennis Norden, British comedian and scriptwriter

The most interesting thing about 'The Woodies' is that they have got 'wood' in their name.
Roy Slaven, Australian entertainer and part of Roy and HG comedy duo, about Australian tennis doubles team players, Todd Woodbridge and Mark Woodford

The fascination of shooting as a sport depends almost wholly on whether you are at the right or wrong end of the gun.
P G Wodehouse (1881-1975), British writer

Pressure is a Messerschmitt up your arse.
Keith Miller (1919-2004), Australian cricketer and WWII fighter plane pilot. Response by Miller to a question from Michael Parkinson on pressure on the cricket field.

I'm not here right now. I'm probably out...LBW to Terry Alderman.
Graham Gooch, English cricket captain, is said to have had this as his phone message when the Australian bowler was having a successful season

The Two Ronnies

The man who invented the zip fastener was today honoured with a lifetime peerage. He will now be known as the Lord of the Flies.

The toilets at a local police station have been stolen. Police say they have nothing to go on.

In a packed programme tonight we will be talking to an out-of-work contortionist who says he can no longer make ends meet.

The prime minister held a meeting with the cabinet today. He also spoke to the bookcase and argued with the chest of drawers.

A cement mixer collided with a prison van on the Kingston Bypass. Motorists are asked to be on the lookout for sixteen hardened criminals.

Following the dispute with the domestic servants' union at Buckingham Palace today, the Queen, a radiant figure in a white silk gown and crimson robe, swept down the main staircase and through the hall. She then dusted the cloakroom and vacuumed the lounge.

We'll continue our investigation into the political beliefs of nudists. We've already noticed a definite swing to the left.

George Mumble, the home county's most henpecked husband, died today. By the terms of his will, his ashes will be scattered all over his wife's new living room carpet.

After a series of crimes in the Glasgow area, Chief Inspector McTavish has announced that he's looking for a man with one eye. If he doesn't find him, he's going to use both eyes.

Tomorrow we will be talking to women who like Nicholas Parsons. And also to a parson who likes knickerless women.

Finally, there's a report from the team who've been investigating the social habits of Mr and Mrs Average. Unfortunately, Mr Average was not at home. He'd slipped down to Brighton with Mrs Well-Above Average.

The marvellous thing about a joke with double meaning is that it can only mean one thing.

From the moment I picked your book up until I laid it down I was convulsed with laughter. Someday I intend reading it.
Groucho Marx

Work

McJob: a low-pay, low-prestige, low-dignity, low-benefit, no-future job in the service sector.
Douglas Coupland, Canadian author

Hacker: Shred that document. No-one must ever be able to find it again.
Bernard: In that case, Minister, I think it's better that I file it.
Yes Minister

He took the job on two conditions. The first was that he didn't have a title. The second was that he never be required to have pot plants in his office.
Gary Pemberton, Australian businessman, about his favourite employee's working conditions

I'll run the company, you go to the cocktail parties.
Gary Pemberton, about his antipathy to business networking

A woman's work is never delegated.
Basil Fawlty to his wife Sybil, *Fawlty Towers*

I hate housework. You make the beds, you do the dishes—and six months later you have to start all over again.
Joan Rivers, American comedian

The trouble with Freud is that he never played the Glasgow Empire Saturday night.
Ken Dodd, British comedian

Committee—a group of men who keep minutes and waste hours.
Milton Berle, American comedian

Meetings are indispensable when you don't want to do anything.
John Kenneth Galbraith, American economist

Just because you've got a bit of form on a country track, doesn't mean you can win the Melbourne Cup.
George Pell, Australian cardinal, in 2005 about his chances of becoming the next Pope

If it's a good script I'll do it. And if it's a bad script, and they pay me enough, I'll do it.
George Burns (1896-1996), American comedian

If the only tool you have is a hammer, you tend to see every problem as a nail.
Abraham Maslow (1908-1970), American psychologist

Retire? Retire to what? I already fish and play golf.
Julius Boros (1920-94), American golfer

A psychiatrist is a man who goes to the Folies Bergère and looks at the audience.
Mervyn Stockwood (1913-95), English bishop

A critic is a man who knows the way but can't drive the car.
Kenneth Tynan (1927-80), English theatre critic

I'm not feeling too well. I need a doctor immediately. Quick, call the nearest golf course.
Groucho Marx (1890-1977), American comedian and actor

Hard work never killed anybody, but why take a chance?
Edgar Bergen (1903-78), American ventriloquist

Working for Warner Bros is like fucking a porcupine—it's a hundred pricks against one.
Wilson Mizner (1876-1933), American screenwriter

Britain has invented a new missile. It's called the civil servant— it doesn't work and it can't be fired.
Sir Walter Walker (1912-2001), English general

Zsa Zsa Gabor

I've been married to a communist and a fascist, and neither of them would take out the garbage.

Marriage is the first step towards divorce.

The quickest way to make a million? Marry it.

I never hated a man enough to give his diamonds back.

I want a man who is kind and understanding. Is that too much to ask of a millionaire?

I know nothing about sex because I was always married.

Macho doesn't prove mucho.

The only person who left the Iron Curtain wearing it.
Oscar Levant (1906-72), American musician and actor

Zsa Zsa Gabor is a wonderful housekeeper. Every time she gets a divorce, she keeps the house.
Henry Youngman (1906-98), American comedian

You can calculate Zsa Zsa Gabor's age by the rings on her fingers.

The Vietnam war finally ended in an agreement neither side intended to honour. It was like one of Zsa Zsa Gabor's weddings.

Zsa Zsa Gabor got married as a one-off and it was so successful she turned it into a series.
Bob Hope (1903-2003), American comedian and actor

Last Words

I told you I was ill.
Spike Milligan

I demand a second opinion.
Spike Milligan (as an alternative to the above)

Jesus Christ, is that the time already?
Billy Connolly

You're standing on my balls.
Billy Connolly (in very small letters)

You can be sure of one thing, I shall treat him as an equal.
Gough Whitlam, when asked about how he would meet his maker

I know this beach like the back of my hand.
Harold Holt (1908-67), Australian prime minister, who drowned at Portsea (VIC) on the day he said these words

He never grew up, but he never stopped growing.
Arthur C Clarke, English science fiction writer

May my husband rest in peace till I get there.
Dame Edna Everage, Australian housewife superstar

Here lies my wife: here let her lie!
Now she's at rest, and so am I.
John Dryden (1631-1700), English poet, for his wife

He was an average guy who could carry a tune.
Bing Crosby (1903-77)

My work is done, why wait?
George Eastman (1854-1932)

I can't eat what I want to eat, drink what I want to drink, do what I want to do or go where I want to go. Son, what is the point of it?
Kerry Packer

Wait a second.
Madame de Pompadour (1721-64) on her deathbed. She wanted to apply rouge to her cheeks, and asked God to oblige which he apparently did

God damn the whole friggin' world and everyone in it but you, Carlotta.

Here lies W C Fields. I would rather be living in Philadelphia.
W C Fields (1880-1946)

Leave the shower curtain on the inside of the tub.
Conrad Hilton (1887-1979). When asked if he had any words of wisdom to leave for the world
I am just going outside and may be some time.
Captain Oates (d 1912)

Excuse my dust.
Dorothy Parker

Never felt better.
Douglas Fairbanks Sr (1883-1939)

Together again.
Gracie Allen and George Burns

It was a great game.
Bing Crosby (1903-77)
After sinking his final putt during a game in Spain, Crosby turned to the spectators and acknowledged their applause saying, 'It was a great game'. He collapsed while walking to the clubhouse. A doctor tried, unsuccessfully, to resuscitate him.

My only regret in life is that I did not drink more champagne.
Lord Keynes' dying words

Do not walk on the grass.
Peter Ustinov

Over my dead body.
George S Kaufman

Here lies Groucho Marx … and lies and lies and lies. PS He never kissed an ugly girl.
Groucho Marx

At last she sleeps alone.
Suggested by Robert Benchley to a promiscuous actress who asked him for an appropriate epitaph

He was a complete tosser.
Tony Banks (1943-2006), Labour minister

I am bored with it all.
Winston Churchill (reported in *New York Times*)

My wallpaper and I are fighting a duel to the death. One or other of us has got to go.
Oscar Wilde, on his deathbed in a Paris hotel

Alas, I am dying beyond my means.
Oscar Wilde, as he sipped champagne on his deathbed

I'm sorry doctor, but I fear I'm going to bother you now.
Pierre Lanson, French champagne maker, aged 97. Dying words to his doctor while drinking a glass of champagne

That's all, folks!
Mel Blanc